BY THE SAME AUTHOR

Published by E. P. DUTTON & CO., INC.

FROM A WRITER'S NOTEBOOK

FROM A WRITER'S NOTEBOOK

By

Van Wyck Brooks

E. P. DUTTON & COMPANY, INC.

NEW YORK, 1958

Library of Congress Catalog Card Number: 58-5066

CONTENTS

FOREWORD

A few of these notes have appeared in earlier books of mine, while others have been printed in *The Nation* and *The New York Times Book Review;* but most of them are published here for the first time.

FROM A WRITER'S NOTEBOOK

I

ON THE MARGIN

IT is only the instructed soul who represents the present. The crowd is the soul of the future in the body of the past.

*
* *

What we call insincerity is the expression of thoughts that do not go to the bottom of our own minds.

*
* *

Nothing is so soothing to our self-esteem as to find our bad traits in our forbears. It seems to absolve us from them.

*
* *

It is not easy by sheer inertia to sink to the lower depths. In order to sink, as well as to rise, a well-organized person has to work, for he has to violate all manner of instincts which it is easier to satisfy. The line of least resistance is to float on a dead level.

*
* *

Earnest people are often people who habitually look on the serious side of things that have no serious side.

*
* *

How few people are able to praise without appearing to patronize, even when they sincerely admire.

*
* *

Nothing is sadder than the consequences of having worldly standards without worldly means.

*
* *

Cant is moral assumption without moral feeling.

*
* *

A man who has the courage of his platitudes is always a successful man. The instructed man is ashamed to pronounce in an orphic manner what everybody knows, and because he is silent people think he is making fun of them. They like a man who expresses their own superficial thoughts in a manner that appears to be profound. This enables them to feel that they are themselves profound.

*
* *

The Pharisees. They have all the virtues and their consciousness of it takes the bloom off them all.

*
* *

The Radio. In a moment of inadvertence the radio was permitted to carry on of itself. Eternal vigilance is the price of freedom from the natural habits of this invention.

*
* *

There are some people who take a fierce delight in doing what they do not want to do.

There are other people who have the worst possible time doing what they know they should not do.

*
* *

Irony is the mortar with which one fills the space between the partial and the universal.

*
* *

Epigrams are truly like coins. There are very few whose image and superscription are not obliterated if we carry them long enough in our mental pockets.

*
* *

Is it possible that sharks and rattlesnakes have nightmares in their sleep, in which they are obliged to feel they are something else, and then wake up again to the delicious realization that they still have their jaws and rattles?

*
* *

Fabre's books on insects,—why do they so fascinate us? Because of the ghastly sidelights they throw on human life, the sinister relief into which they cast our own instincts and habits.

*
* *

A generation lasts thirty years, or five, as we say in America. Who form the next generation? Not those who bask complacently in this. One has to be partly at odds with the *zeitgeist* of one's age if one wishes to contribute to the building of another.

*
* *

My friend C.F. met at Carlsbad one of the Hollywood movie magnates. He had himself just seen a fine performance of Lessing's *Minna von Barnhelm,* and he told the great man that he should make a picture of it. They talked for a while of other matters, and then, as they were parting, the magnate said, "Now what about this fellow Lessing? When you see him, ask him how much he wants for his play."

*
* *

We do not fear a single thing
Except our relatives,

say the elephants in chorus in the Ramayana. These elephants lived in ancient India, many centuries ago, but evidently there were good Freudians even in those days.

*
* *

We Americans have always thought either too much or too little of ourselves, as we have thought either too much or too little of Europe. As in the nineteenth century we thought too much of Europe, so we are in danger of thinking too little of it now.

*
* *

Care as we may about the future of the world, there is something in us that does not care if it involves our own discomfort. "I won't be there to see it," we say to ourselves with relief when we think of the inevitable consequences of some tendency of our time that we find either tragic or distasteful. After me the deluge.

*
* *

Gibbon observes that the ancient Germans, when they were summoned to a public meeting, would lag behind the appointed time in order to show their independence. This trait was still more marked, according to Parkman, among the American Indians of Pontiac's time.

Similarly, my friend X and other editorial potentates rattle their papers on their desks for ten or twenty minutes, before they admit their suppliants, in order to show how important and busy they are. Henceforth I shall think of editors as ancient Germans.

*
* *

Travel becomes uninteresting, someone has remarked, in exact proportion to its rapidity. It is certainly true,

in any case, that all the great travel books were written
when travelling was uncomfortable and slow. Travel-
lers had sharper impressions then because they had to
suffer for them. Discomfort keeps the mind alive and
awake, whereas modern ways of travelling breed inertia in the mind.

In Freya Stark's Arabia and Persia, travel is still
uncomfortable and slow. That is one reason for the
great excellence of so many books about those countries.

*

* *

Most idealizations of the past spring from a tendency of
the idealizer to identify himself with the great ones of
the past. He says to himself, If I had lived in the thir-
teenth century, I would have been a cathedral-builder,
or I would have been a cardinal or a duchess or a
Thomas Aquinas. I would have been one of the happy
few who formed the epoch, historically speaking, never
one of the millions who were clods or swineherds. I
would have been a creator of the famous unity of the
Middle Ages, a unity which was due to the fact that
non-conformity springs from thought and only a handful were permitted to use their minds.

*
* *

The salesman is the priest of our civilization. No matter how heavily weighted his recommendations may be, there are large elements of the population who take them at face value. They believe all they are told of the habits of "these distinguished people," and every soap is the best if the salesman says so. They adopt his sales-patter as their normal language, and they no more think of questioning the validity of this than the faithful of the Church of Rome question their Latin.

*
* *

As a rule, people who take a low view of human nature feel that they themselves are superior beings, but I have noticed that, more often than not, they are in reality rather mean men. They would be surprised if they were told that what they see in others is, in fact, what others see in them.

II

READERS AND WRITERS

THERE are two great categories of writers, those who are solicited from the outside, prompted by the suggestions of others, and those who are prompted entirely from within, who have "one tap-root that goes down deep," like Willa Cather's old Nebraska farmer.

*

* *

How many literary careers suggest the fabled serpent that eats its tail. By good work a writer earns a reputation; then his reputation earns him a lucrative job; then the lucrative job destroys the reputation. So the serpent in the end consumes itself.

*

* *

As everyone must know, Alfred Russel Wallace discovered simultaneously with Darwin the origin of species. Darwin had been warned that he would be forestalled, and when Wallace sent him his first sketch Darwin had to wrestle with his angel, tempted as he was to put forth a prior claim. In the end the papers of both were published jointly. The story illustrates the kind of coincidence that every writer expects when he chooses a subject. No sooner do we project a book and begin to write it than we fancy the whole world has chosen the same subject and is secretly working to get ahead of us.

*

* *

All kinds of writers exist in every country, but the writers who are most interesting are those in whom the country differs most from others, in whom one feels the uniqueness of the country. Who would wish Stendhal less French than he is, or Fielding or Dickens less English, or *Oblomov* less Russian? Is that not largely the quality we seek in foreign literature and the quality that foreigners seek among us?

*

* *

Whoever is accustomed to reading with a definite object in mind cannot long endure desultory reading. An object acts as a magnet attracting, in all one reads, the facts and the ideas that are relevant to it, and this creates an excitement in the mind that makes all purposeless reading tame and insipid. And yet what a pity this is, for it is desultory reading that develops one's taste. It is fortunate that when we are young we are unfocussed.

*

* *

How many books can any man read? A supposedly well-informed journalist has written that Hitler undoubtedly read most of the 7000 military books in his library. So Lawrence of Arabia was said to have read at Oxford most of the 40,000 books in the library of his college. So Thomas Wolfe allegedly devoured 20,000 books or so. Wolfe obviously pictured himself as Eugene Gant in *Look Homeward, Angel,* "pulling books out of a thousand shelves and reading like a madman . . . He read insanely, by the hundreds, the thousands, the ten thousands." How tiresome, all this, and how untrue. People speak of these things very much at their ease. For the last twenty years I have been obliged to read on an average six or seven hours a day. I have certainly read far more than these others have had time for, in the short periods referred to, and how many books have I read in these twenty years? Something less than 6,000, I think, less than a book a day.

*
* *

Every writer who has lived long and passed through several phases acquires a public that is attached to each one of these phases; and each of these publics thinks that the writer ought to remain in the phase that it finds sympathetic. Once a literary radical, he should always remain one; once an authority on this or that, he should never be anything else. Every one of these publics is determined that he shall not grow an inch beyond the phase in which it liked him, and no matter how self-consistent he is or how natural his growth has been, there will always be some public that regards him as a traitor.

*
* *

Intensity always prevails. Whoever possesses intensity is bound to conquer other minds, whatever the nature of the intensity, angelic or diabolic, positive or negative, minor or major, human or inhuman.

*
* *

It is difficult to understand living writers because they are involved in our own problems, which we cannot solve for ourselves.

*
*   *

It is not that the French are not profound, but they all express themselves so well that we are led to take their geese for swans.

*
*   *

Some writers have a tendentious importance that is quite apart from any intrinsic importance. I can think of two living writers, one of whom cannot write and the other has nothing to say, yet who, in the literary history of our time, will have their place, for they represent tendencies of feeling, characteristic of the time, which the more important writers have not expressed at all.

*
*   *

The Psychology of the Literary "Cult." The devotees of an author,—I mean the kind of author who has devotees, who is the centre of a cult,—differ from those who admire him in the ordinary way. They differ in that they share the defects of their idol. By means of the idol they redress these defects and find excuses for their own shortcomings.

*
* *

The Genteel Tradition. This phrase has had too long a run. It has been stretched in so many directions that it is as lifeless as an old elastic. One cannot bear too heavily on suggestive phrases, and one grows heartily sick of these phrases when they have been used three times. Besides, the writers who use this phrase confound the noble with the genteel. They will be calling Marcus Aurelius genteel next.

*
* *

A seed catalogue,—Stumpp and Walter's,—says that if you wish to develop new and beautiful varieties, you must save the weak seedlings. The strongest seedlings are pretty certain to run true to type. Using the words "weak" and "strong" as most people use them, is this not generally true of writers also?

*
* *

With all that can be said of Kipling,—and much must be said, for he was a great writer,—we cannot forget that, in his biblical argot, he invented the thieves' slang of imperialism.

*
* *

Stevenson always wrote as if he were talking with a woman who admired him. It is this that gives him his air of conscious heroism.

*
* *

One has to be interested in England to enjoy Anthony Trollope, but to enjoy Balzac all one needs is to be interested in life.

*
* *

Nietzsche convinced every Pomeranian puppy that he was a mastiff. He made all his readers feel that they were aristocrats without being or doing anything to support the assumption.

*
* *

Regarding the "creative writing" courses in our colleges, one must add that they tend to destroy the audience of literature. They do so by promoting into writers, and often opinionative writers, the susceptible but uncreative persons who might otherwise be the best readers.

*
* *

A writer is important not by the amount of territory he enters or claims, but by the amount he colonizes. Tolstoy and Dickens fill all the space they occupy. They do not merely lie, like Milton's Satan, full many a rood prone on the flood.

*
* *

There are writers who, as writers, ought to die, and the only way to contribute to this end is not to mention them.

*
* *

This writer reminds me of the Pasha's remark, in Kinglake's *Eöthen*, marvelling over the ways of the Europeans, "Whirr! Whirr! All by wheels! Whiz! Whiz! All by steam!"

*
* *

B's writing always reminds me of a man skating. He seems to be skating all over that beautiful smooth ice, in graceful circles, but never getting anywhere, not even cutting the ice.

*
* *

I hear a young person brightly referring to the "Greenwich Village quarter of Paris, whatever that is." How times change! Only a few months ago, one would say, the Latin Quarter was the standard phrase for these regions in every city on the planet.

*
* *

But, speaking of Greenwich Village, how does it happen that artists and writers have always felt so at home there? It is perhaps because, in the modern American city, this region remains a fragment of Europe, or of an America that was European (for all our older cities in earlier times were European colonial towns). America is only just becoming the blood-homeland of the artist mind, and it still feels a little shivery and lonesome in the great out-doors of megalopolis.

*
* *

A.E. once quoted to me in a letter a phrase from the Bhagavad-Gita, "Let the motive for action be in the action itself and not in the event." That a man's opinions may have consequences, that literature itself has consequences of a very important kind, is naturally perhaps the first of a writer's convictions; but he must feel that he as a writer must disregard this. For Renan was right when he said, "To be able to think freely, one must feel that what one writes will have no consequences."

*
*   *

I do not believe in golden ages, and may heaven smite the praiser of times past who tries to shame the present with examples of what was never, surely, his own past. The so-called golden ages are merely times when men know how to use their powers and make more of their lives than at other times.

*
*   *

"The women lived it, the men wrote about it," Rudolph Ruzicka said one day of the German romantic movement. This is true of all literary movements.

*
*   *

"Nowadays everything grows old in a few hours; reputation fades, a work passes away in a moment. Everybody writes; nobody reads seriously." How often,

in the twentieth century, one hears this lament! It
was uttered by Chateaubriand in 1836.

*
* *

Mannerism is the sign of a second-rate mind; pride in
mannerism is the sign of a third-rate mind.

*
* *

They are like the ghosts of iridescent lizards, those
wondrous unborn thoughts we almost catch but that
slip back into our unconscious before we are actually
aware of them. Such are the "fallings from us—
vanishings" to which Wordsworth refers in his great
ode.

*
* *

"Seeing Shelley plain" is not always rewarding. Arthur
Davison Ficke, the poet, told me that when he left
Harvard, on a voyage round the world, he stopped at
Athens. Entering the breakfast room in the dingy little
Hotel Minerva, he heard a voice saying, "Good morn-
ing, Mr. Ficke"; and there, sitting at a small table,
was George Santayana, who had been one of his pro-
fessors. The next morning Santayana exclaimed, "Good

morning, Mr. James," as the face of William James appeared at the door. James had come to spend a month in Athens. The two philosophers invited Ficke to take his meals with them, and I asked him what these great men had talked about. Mainly golf, he said,— one of them played golf and the other didn't. They did not bark at one another, as the officers barked in *The Red Badge of Courage*, while the soldier Henry Fleming listened to their talk. But neither did these two Shelleys utter what Stephen Crane's soldier expected to hear as he listened for "some great inner historical things."

*

* *

Mrs. B. tells me that she dined in Cambridge once with both Josiah Royce and William James. As Royce mumbled and bumbled along, James turned to her and said, "Royce has a God,—doesn't love him. If *I* had a God, wouldn't I love him!"

How much of William James is not in that.

*

* *

One must take Veblen with more than one grain of salt. People are always willing today to credit a mean motive but find it difficult to credit a magnanimous

one, and Veblen has contributed to form this frame
of mind. Consider what he said of "conspicuous waste"
and think at the same time of Mary Magdalen's box
of precious ointment. Could anything have been more
conspicuous, and was it waste? Then I remember
Charles Beard's love for large airy spacious rooms
that might also have been called wasteful, and conspicuously so. For no one really needs any such thing.
Charles Beard was an admiring colleague of Veblen,
but John Stuart Mill interprets for us Beard's far from
Veblenian feeling about this matter. Mill had found,
as he says in his autobiography, that a grand and
spacious room can have an enlarging effect upon the
mind. "There is nothing like space. It enlarges the
ideas," said old Prince Saracinesca in the well-known
novel; and of how much this is true that is sometimes
called waste.

*
* *

In her study of Alexander Pope, Edith Sitwell speaks of
the willow under which he sat so often in his Twickenham garden. Cuttings of this willow were sent by
Pope's successors in the Twickenham house to various
parts of Europe, and especially to the Empress Cath-
erine of Russia; and Edith Sitwell says of this tree,

which died in 1901, "It is said to be the ancestor of all the weeping willows in our gardens." If that is true, Pope's willow must have more descendants than any other tree in history except the Tree of Life. For, according to the poet Bryant, in one of his published orations, it was the ancestor also of all the Connecticut willows, or at least all the willows on the Housatonic River. The first president of Columbia University, Samuel Johnson of Stratford, Connecticut, called upon Pope on one occasion, and the poet gave him also a cutting from this willow which he planted in his garden on the river. All the other willows spread from this.

Of all trees the willow is perhaps the most philoprogenitive. Benjamin Franklin raised willows at home from the withes of an old "dead" basket which he had picked up in a gutter in France. My friend Joel Spingarn planted an avenue a mile long, lined on both sides with willows that had all grown from cuttings of a single tree.

*

* *

How quintessentially Southern was Poe's imagination! Anyone can see this who spends an hour, for instance, in the Bonaventure Cemetery at Savannah. Who could forget an alley there, flanked by ancient live-oak trees, with streamers of grey moss overhanging the path, leading to the lichen-covered tomb of a long-dead senator and his daughter, with the waves of the "sounding sea" breaking behind it? Nothing could more completely evoke the quality of Poe. There are similar scenes in the Magnolia Cemetery, which Poe must have visited when he was in Charleston.

*
* *

Several literary types have vanished from the world under the stresses and strains of the world-war epoch, the bookman, for instance, and the man of letters, rightly so called, types that existed everywhere fifty years ago. I do not mean the parlour dispenser of "art appreciation," who was really a sort of parody of the artist as critic, but the superior type that was represented in England by Saintsbury, for one, and with us by Huneker and a number of others. These were the men, ubiquitous once, who followed the by-paths of literature and art and communicated a taste for them as a mode of pure enjoyment, and, like the old Trelawny type of literary adventurer, they have disappeared with the pressure of modern living.

So also the by-paths they followed have been left

untrodden. Life has become too difficult and our atmosphere has become too harsh for these types to survive in America or even in Europe, although one still finds them there as one finds tinkers on Irish roads who recall the days of *Lavengro* and *The Romany Rye*. So one sees on Dublin streets or even London streets the Yellow Book dandy and the threadbare author who carry the mind back to Max Beerbohm and the novels of George Gissing. But in general these types are as lost and forgotten, in literature and life, as the days of the "Household Poets" or the days when Thackeray wrote novels "in the gentlemanly interest." It is just as Huneker said, in the early twenties, before he died, "Seven devils of war and woe . . . and hatred, murder and rapine have driven forth the gentle arts from the House of Life."

The literary temperature is too inclement for these types now,—that is to say, the prevailing spirit of the age, for, as Taine pointed out, according to the temperature, so is the selection that takes place among the species of talent. Some species prove abortive that would have thriven in a warmer air and that may thrive again at some time in the future: they are extinguished or fail to develop when the customs of the moment and the public mind repress them or close the outlets which they require. William James, in one of his essays, followed a cognate line of thought when he spoke of the kinds of genius that are at odds with their surroundings, that are condemned to be ineffective because "some previous genius of a different strain has warped the community away" from them. Putting together the kinds of genius that have moulded the mind of our time with the spiritual climate that a world-war epoch has created, one can easily understand why these types have been pushed to the wall.

*

* *

While certain types disappear, others continue to exist, but as it were behind the scenes, and one of these types in America I would describe as the wits and sages who are ignored in the welter of our literary life. John Jay Chapman, in one of his letters, says that as late as 1930 the editor of *Life* had never heard of him,—though this editor prided himself on his general awareness; and Chapman was the author of thirty books as well as a very conspicuous man, in the highest degree turbulent and picturesque. If he was little known, it is only natural that so many others have lived like treetoads on a leaf, scarcely visible even to their neighbours,—those often shy recessive men, frequently perceptive, who have lived in "pro-

fessors' houses" all over the country. (For I think of
Willa Cather's Professor St. Peter as, in some fashion,
the type of them all.) Arthur Ryder, the Sanskrit
scholar, and William Ellery Leonard, the poet, were
actual variations of the type, like Frank Moore Colby,
who would have been famous as a wit if the "temperature" had been different in his time and place. Who
knows much or anything of the Michigan professor
Charles Horton Cooley, the author of the collection of
aphorisms called *Life and the Student,* and what could
be better in their way than some of these?—

When we are perplexed we project the disorder of our
minds in a belief that the world is anarchical.

When one is trying to write a book most of the work is
done not in the actual writing, but in the unconscious proc-
esses, which move obscurely by day and night. It is inter-
ference with these, through a sort of subterranean competi-
tion, not mere loss of time, that makes other responsibilities
detrimental.

Violent revolutions are made by people who have no chance
to try out their ideas.

A man may write on Love and Art and Peace and what
not, but he will write to little purpose unless he has, behind
it all, a natural ferocity. We like ease in a book, but
only such as has been won by struggle. We should not care
for the cathedral if we did not sense the quarry behind it.

In short, to care for a man's writing, one must feel
the tension in it, "some sense of the struggle that life

is," as Cooley puts it. I would say, for instance, that in Charles Lamb's gaiety one feels the mental insecurity that constantly beset him. Was it not this that gave Lamb his preëminence over the easy-going tribe of the "familiar" writers?

*

*   *

When one thinks of the newspapers of fifty years ago, with their felt classical allusions and regard for style,— the *New York Tribune,* for instance, and the *Evening Post,*—one can almost say that nineteenth-century journalism constantly aspired to the condition of literature. One may add that, in the same degree, after about 1900, literature as constantly tended to the condition of journalism.

*

*   *

Literature, properly speaking, has three dimensions,— breadth, depth and elevation. Most great writers have had these three dimensions, but few modern writers have more than two. Many have breadth, some have depth, and there are numbers who combine these two dimensions; but how very few at present have elevation! Three generations ago, this was perhaps the chief dimension of writers. Now the time has come round for it again, and I hope it will not be abused.

*
* *

Dr. Alexis Carrel said that what the world needs is a "high council of doctors" to rule it for its good. So H. G. Wells always said that the world should be ruled by engineers, and no doubt the West Point men feel that the world should be ruled by a General Staff. I know I have a tendency to feel that the world should be ruled by writers; but, though Goethe was a good administrator, I do not forget the remark of Frederick the Great. He said the worst thing he could do to punish a province was to sentence it to be governed by a man of letters. No, let writers rule by writing, as they do rule, even at present; for "Imagination governs mankind," as a practical man, Napoleon, said,—and who rules the imagination more than writers?

III

IN OUR TIME

As I enter the room in Greenwich Village, the first object that catches my eye is a coloured print of Breughel's "Icarus," and it strikes me at once that this is a symbol of a young man's state of mind in the nineteen-fifties. Every generation has favourite pictures that symbolize its desires and fears, and this picture of a boy falling out of the sky in the presence of indifferent onlookers has obviously in our time a special meaning. Icarus, in any case, is a theme that fascinates our luckless age, the theme of two of the sculptures, for instance, in the Metropolitan Museum show of American sculpture in 1951. There Hélène Sardeau's "Icarus" reigned over the rest. Breughel's picture has been the subject of two German treatises in the last few years. It is also the theme of one of Auden's poems.

In this poem the ploughman on the bank unconcernedly goes on with his work while the boy who has lost his wings falls into the river. He "may have heard the splash, the forsaken cry," Auden says, "but

for him it was not an important failure"; and to whom
are such things important in an age of genocide when
human life has become so expendable and cheap?
There are no more parades for young men who are
shipped off to war, nor does anyone think any more
of calling them heroes in a world of existentialism
in which all the great causes are dead, we are told,
and the individual is lost in a universal Bigness. Big
wars, big armies, big offices and bigger cities. The
wings the boy has lost are now on the motor-cars; and
this is the age of the "hot-rod kids" who say, "I'm
going to die anyway. Who cares?"

*
* *

"Time-Provincialism." Half the energy of Americans
up to the world-war epoch was spent in trying to
escape from provinciality. They did their best to place
themselves at Matthew Arnold's "centre." But provinciality of place is not the only provinciality. There
is also time-provincialism, in Professor Whitehead's
phrase. ("Men can be provincial in time as well as in
place.") And have not those who have jumped out of
Mencken's famous "boobery" jumped very often into
this frying-pan? Americans, more than other people,
feel that they must be up to the minute, as if this

last minute were more important than any of the great realities of life and death. How many of them repeat Daumier's phrase, "One must be of one's time": how few can have said with Ingres, "But suppose my time is wrong?"

This is not the only period, nor are we the only people who have been aware of the importance of "living in the present." But there is no doubt that people who felt this in former times were also aware of their forbears and of the past. It was their reading of the Bible and the classics that saved them from time-provincialism; and, having, in consequence, equipoise and a standard of value, they knew their present better than we know ours.

*

*   *

A publisher in England, advertising a new novel, says, "It contains no obscenities in the new American tradition," and I am wondering how long this tradition is going to last and why it thrives especially in our country. It is understandable that the modern mind requires discord with its harmony, that the beautiful must be "damned beautiful" to be mentioned at all, and I am aware of the prudery that dogged the American literary mind in the generation when I was grow-

ing up. But how long does this kind of reaction perform a real function?—and does one not feel now a
kind of monotonous adolescence in our use of the
cloacal word and the scene it evokes? When a character in a recent story, referring to the setting sun at
sea, says it "looks like a big red behind being lowered
into a bathtub," I think of some of the images that
scene called up before Buck Mulligan spoke of the
"snotgreen sea." In countless minds this phrase of
Joyce deflated for all time the association of the sea
with majesty and greatness that Homer had kept alive
for two thousand years, and, while this may have been
called for at the moment, deflation ever since has
been virtually the rule in literary usage. And how
tiresome in this flatness, this dull concentration on the
mean,—as tiresome as the witless grin that seems to be
obligatory in the photographs of public persons nowadays.

*
* *

Originally "sweetness and light" was a phrase of the
author of *Gulliver's Travels*. These qualities were the
"two noblest of things," said Swift, who was anything
but a fatuous man; but would anyone dare so to call
them now? They have become a byword and a hiss-

ing, as if bitterness and darkness were better than sweetness and light; and beside the granitic self-protective disillusionment of our time these words are as ineffectual as spray against a sea-wall. They are as obsolete as old-fashioned phrases like "a sound-hearted sailor" and "a free-hearted soldier," phrases that stood for syntheses and seem to belong to a foreign tongue in our day of analysis and the analytic mind.

And, indeed, how could people be expected to admire these traits when they feel that to go "soft" is to open themselves to destruction? But, although we cannot accept them now, must be not admit that they are superior attributes of the well and the strong? Surely to be able to take an enlightened harmonious view of life is the end-product of all psychotherapy, and can it be denied that in any scale of values "sweetness and light" are precisely what Swift called them? Taken together, they constitute almost the perfect phrase for any truly desirable historical epoch,—for instance, the Periclean age, as we like to think it was,—just as the phrase "a Christian gentleman," everywhere nowadays used in contempt, is almost the perfect phrase for a desirable person. (Don Quixote, or the Vicar of Wakefield, or Colonel Newcome.) But when, at the outset of a modern story, one sees the phrase "a Christian gentleman," one knows what to expect before the story closes,—the kind of scoundrel who has all the attributes that are commonly associated at present with "sweetness and light."

This phrase flourished in the days when the Sistine Madonna and Murillo's Immaculate Conception were the world's favourite pictures. It was spoiled already in my childhood, and I do not expect to see it flourish again in a day when "Hell" Breughel and Picasso reign over minds. But I think we should keep its right of way open,—just as the bronze statue does in Trois Rivières in Quebec that commemorates the "douceur" of the old French bishop. If ours is a demented world, as so many think and say, we should share its emotional life while retaining our reason, as a sane visitor in a mental hospital shares the patients' feelings while maintaining in his own mind the standard of mental health.

What Theodore Dreiser said about manners in *A Traveller at Forty* is relevant in this connection also: "Our early revolt against sham civility has resulted in nothing save the abolition of all civility, which is sickening." The real and the sham sweetness and light have gone out together, as bitterness and darkness have come in. But will not people some day rub their eyes and ask themselves how this "transvaluation of values" ever happened?

*
* *

I observe in Kafka's novels an extensive knowledge of hotels, and this might surely be called a note of our time. How many contemporary novels of all degrees of merit have been written about hotels, from Arnold Bennett's *Imperial Palace* and Sinclair Lewis's *Work of Art* to Vicki Baum and Erich Maria Remarque. This suggests an epoch when all mankind is on the march, shifting like the particles of glass in a kaleidoscope. The hero of one of these novels feels it is "better to drift," as he puts it,—he is living in a refugee hotel in Paris. Why attempt to "build up a bourgeois life again in a century that is falling to pieces"? Why waste energy? It is better to live on the branch.

In American writing the saloon plays the part of the hotel. The saloon, the bar or the "back room" has been central in the novels, stories and plays of the last three generations of American writers, including Bret Harte and Jack London. One recalls the place that McSorley's saloon, painted by John Sloan, played in the Greenwich Village life of the twenties, the place the saloon in general played in the lives of Stephen Crane, John Reed and Edmund Wilson's "Boys in the Back Room." How many of Eugene O'Neill's plays were set in a saloon, along with Charles Jackson's *The Lost Week-*

end, the stories of Dos Passos and Scott Fitzgerald and Hemingway's *The Sun Also Rises.* The bar is undoubtedly what the drawing-room used to be, the favourite locus of the literary imagination.

*
* *

Someone remarks in an English weekly that our poets are now all "dim," and for this I think he makes a plausible case. He attributes this dimness to Eliot's teaching. Eliot has taught them that it is better to be a good minor poet than a bad major one, a notion that, on the face of it, is obviously true.

Yet there is something wrong with this if one wants poetry that is not dim, poetry that is, at least occasionally, major; and is it not true that great work springs from great expectations, even if, almost always, these fall flat? The poets who used to invoke the muse did not ask that lady to encourage them to stay within safe limits, for they were not concerned with "middle flights." They wished, like Milton, to soar above the Aonian mount and asked the muse to support their "adventurous" song.

One could make the same point about human expectations at a time when everyone seeks the safe and sane, when the young are encouraged to look for security while they conform to known rules, taking no chances in the great out-of-bounds. But this will not do either if one wants a life that is not "dim" and great new leaders who can create a future. There were certainly many failures in the days when Plutarch's heroes were held up as models for the young, but there were great moral and intellectual successes also, and it was always said that nothing so stirred the young as to have large demands made upon them. Nobody knows what would have happened if Garibaldi had offered his men good berths, security and comfort, but it is certain that they flocked about him when, like Winston Churchill, he offered them toil and sweat, blood and tears. He offered "neither pay, nor quarters, nor provisions," but "hunger, thirst, forced battles and death," adding, "Let him who loves his country in his heart, and not with his lips only, follow me."

In our shell-shocked post-war world, it is natural that caution should prevail, with small expectations and demands in both poetry and life; for enthusiasm and optimism have proved to be treacherous and our world does not encourage a feeling of adventure. How many of the young now "pant to be of age and then to plunge into the vague, uncharted, fascinating future," as Bernard Berenson says he panted in his childhood when the world seemed open and friendly to every ambition? Feelings of this kind are not to be looked for in the America of our day, yet no one seems to like this "dreary time," this "dismal age," to use the phrases of two acute observers.

There are periods of low vitality, and this no doubt is one of them, when the human reservoir seems to be exhausted, and it is true that life only appears to have possibilities when the tide of vitality is high. The main thing in times like ours is not to lose the sense of the difference between the minor and the major.

*
*   *

With shining faces,—in the morning paper,—the well-known novelist and his daughter and wife set out on a plane for Madrid to see the bullfights, and only the other day I read that Sidney Franklin had opened in California a school for bullfighters. There has also been much in the news about an American girl matador who is following in the steps of this young man from Brooklyn.

How many books, for the rest, have been written in praise of bullfighting since Hemingway created a fashion for this mediæval sport, a sport that was once regarded as on the level of stallion-baiting or the bear-baiting that people gave up in disgust. There was also a game of cat-worrying that rivalled the cock-fights which Mark Twain, in New Orleans, refused to see, the same Mark Twain who expressed his opinion of bullfighting in a story written from the horse's point of view. Even Napoleon's generals, when they invaded Spain, expressed their disapproval of so barbarous a sport, and James Huneker, who said "We prefer the abattoir," continued, in *The New Cosmopolis,* as follows: "The meanest feature is not the slaughter of the mild old cattle but the occasional disembowelment of a horse. The toreadors, matadors, picadors are operatic creatures, more spoiled than Italian tenors and twice as useless." And how speak the English and the French? D. H. Lawrence described bullfighting as "the grandeur of Rome—soiling its breeches," and André Gide said in his Journal, perhaps speaking for his countrymen, "To kill someone because he is angry may be all right, but to anger someone in order to kill him is absolutely criminal. It is in a state of mortal sin that the bull is killed."

It is a violation of some deep instinct in us to separate the aesthetic from the humane, and it cannot be supposed that these writers were unaware of the "art" that justifies the sport in the eyes of so many. Or of the value the sport may have in toughening minds that see themselves in an epoch of world wars as "tumbril bait." But to what could it lead if this fashion went unchecked and no one objected to Hemingway's masculine protest, which resembles in certain ways Theodore Roosevelt's small-boy zest for shooting off animals' heads and breaking their backs? Not that Americans in general have changed in their feeling about bullfights. A friend in Madrid writes to me, "Spaniards, when they see Americans in good seats, keep their eyes on them, knowing that they can soon take their places." Americans in general do not share the convenient theological notion of the Spaniards that, inasmuch as animals have no souls, it does matter what happens to their bodies. We, or our English congeners, invented the S.P.C.A. and seem unlikely to lose the feelings that inspired it; but I think it would be a sad perversion if the literary imagination lost in this matter its touch with the general mind. The Hindu regard for the sacredness of life is much more normal to the writer,—even if sacred cows in myriads wander through India as a consequence of this and sacred monkeys are permitted to befoul the rice-fields. When Abraham Lincoln in his youth pursued a snake through thickets to prevent it from swallowing a frog and saved a fawn's life by scaring it away from a rifle, he was acting in line with the discipline that requires writers to value life on pain of losing the power to recreate it.

How paradoxical is our age that praises both Hemingway's blood-lust and the quixotic humanity of Schweitzer and Gandhi,—Gandhi who removed silkworms from the leaves of a tree that were poisoning them and Schweitzer who rescues earthworms that are scorched by the sun.

*
* *

The writers who are to play a part in the rebuilding of civilization will share some of Schweitzer's reverence for life, the reverence that John Bartram revealed when this old naturalist was filled with compunction over the field-flowers that he had so carelessly mowed. They will understand the feeling of William James about vivisection, that he must somehow pay something back to life for every jet of pain that he was causing. Thomas Hardy wrote in *Tess* a chapter on the pheasants that were wounded to make sport for the English gentry,—after which, he said, the gentry cut him,—and Aldous Huxley and Bertrand Russell are vice-presidents of a society "to stop the sordid and ugly pastime of hunting foxes to death for fun." Pope's essay on the mistreatment of animals might convince one of his goodness of heart if it were not for his ridicule of the "dinnerlessness" and "rags" that he found so delightfully funny in the wretches of Grub Street.

"It has become a custom to call anyone a sentimentalist who is sufficiently civilized to be susceptible to the tender emotions." So says Lord David Cecil somewhere. But unless we cultivate tenderness, what will become of a human world that is now as red as nature in tooth and claw?

*

* *

It is not clear to me how Rasputin's conception of "salvation by sin" differs from our fashionable contemporary Graham Greene's. For is it not implied in Graham Greene's novels that adultery is a prerequisite of sainthood? This was precisely Rasputin's message to the ladies of the Czar's court before the puritanical free-lovers of communism came in. St. Paul rebukes them both in the Epistle to the Romans: "Shall we continue in sin that grace may abound? God forbid."

The average sensual man who takes his adultery plain seems to me closer at least to mental sainthood, for he deceives neither himself nor others; and, as for the conception of original sin and of man as inevitably fallen, how does this fare even in Graham Greene's writings? In his *Journey Without Maps* (1936), he presents the natives of Sierra Leone as invariably kind, courteous and instinctively humane, and his highest tribute to the missionary priests is that they had "a standard of gentleness and honesty equal to the native standard." This must be largely a true report, moreover, for Greene travelled everywhere on foot without weapons of any kind through the African jungle.

Since we are driven to choose again between Saint Augustine and Rousseau, does this not suggest Rousseauism, pure and simple? It tallies with Schweitzer, more or less, with Izak Dineson's *Out of Africa* and with Alan Paton's picture of the black man who is still uncorrupted. One and all corroborate the saying of Ecclesiastes: "Men were made upright, but they have sought out many inventions." That was Rousseau's idea and it enables one to see why Rousseau was the father of liberalism and modern reform. If men were basically evil, who would bother to improve the world instead of giving it up as a bad job at the outset,—as many of the "original sinners" counsel us to do? But with good material to work with, and for, one can do something about the "many inventions."

Unless humanity is intrinsically decent, heaven help the world indeed, for more and more we are going to see man naked. There is no stopping the world's tendency to throw off imposed restraints, the religious authority that is based on the ignorance of the many, the political authority that is based on the knowledge of the few. The time is coming when there will be nothing to restrain men except what they find in their own bosoms; and what hope is there for us then unless it is true that, freed from fear, men are naturally predisposed to be upright and just?

No doubt in Rousseau's "natural man" there is much infantile sadism that is by no means lost when he develops; and Pascal was right in saying that one ought to keep in mind both man's imperfections and his greatness. In our day of sophistication, however, it is taken for a sign that one knows life if one sees evil only, while to see anything else is taken for a sign that one is merely a fresh-water sailor. And who in our day likes to be considered naive? But must we believe that Saint Augustine, the great provincial, knew more about men and life than other thinkers? Did he know more than Grotius, who established the science of international law on a basic belief in the natural decency of people? Or than Thomas Jefferson, who said that, because some were unfaithful, he could not act as if all men were so. When Jefferson remarked, "I would rather be the victim of occasional infidelities than relinquish my general confidence in the honesty of men," he was expressing at the same time a well-founded point of view and a truly humane and desirable notion of living.

A century or more ago a "Satanic mania" throve in England resembling our obsession that mankind is rotten to the core. As Bulwer-Lytton's novel *Pelham* is supposed to have put an end to this, I suggest that we offer a prize for a *Pelham* of our time.

*

* *

I am the less inclined to like the idea of original sin because it was once the dominant idea in America and because our literature had its real beginning when we got rid of this idea. A century and a half ago the Calvinistic view was the governing view in our leading intellectual circles, when books like Owen's *Indwelling Sin* were the staple of reading in New England, at least, and life was regarded as mainly a preparation for death. Emerson said that all thoughts were "directed on death" in his childhood and all the terrors of theology were employed to reinforce them. Children were "little fallen wretches," they were "shapen in iniquity," they were victims of "total depravity" and "more hateful than vipers"; and theology, as Channing said, laboured without ceasing to crush the will of mankind to believe in itself. Oliver Wendell Holmes, who satirized this faith in *The One-Hoss Shay,* knew as a doctor how dangerous were its notions and how they poisoned and paralyzed the spirit of man, and the literary movement in New England began when Channing, among others, with his confidence in man, aroused the creative faculties in so many people. Who remembered then that men were "fallen" and that their motives and efforts were "worthless" and "vain"? —and why has this period been called a little Renaissance? Because it was a time of rebirth after another Middle Ages; and what marked it was what marked the great Renaissance when Ulrich von Hutten said, "It is good to be alive."

So it does not amuse me to see critics nowadays rebuilding the "one-hoss shay" under our eyes, trying to revive the point of view that characterized the American mind when it was still impotent, shackled, dormant and sterile. There are good reasons, I well know, in a time of war and suffering, why "most of us" are "eschatologists," as Lional Trilling puts it, referring to a large group of his fellow-critics; but we should see this as one of the notes *of* a time of war and suffering, not as something intrinsically admirable, desirable or true. Who expects anyone to say "It is good to be alive" in "the worst time I've ever heard about," as Hemingway recently called our epoch, a time when people are almost obliged to dwell on death and "last things" and the tragic seems almost the only true note to strike? But how far must we go in for self-abasement?—and can we not at least remember that the great moments of humankind have been those in which men believed in their own powers? It was the great day of the Persian poets when Hafiz and Saadi, for instance, escaped from the Mohammedan fatalism that had much in common with our old Calvinism, and, similarly, when one asks much of men, believing in their powers, they are apt to respond in proportion to this expectation. And that is the trouble with the idea of original sin. Whoever suggested hanging a dog when one gives him an ill name knew that, in these conditions, he is willing to be hanged; and is this not the case with men as well? When they are told incessantly that they are "false," "fickle," "corrupt" and "depraved" and that the world they live in is disgusting and hopeless, are they likely to rouse themselves and live, as we say, creatively, or, rather, to shrink into themselves, dejected and beaten?

and so to ask of oneself.

This is a question to bear in mind in the face of a critical movement that glories in its revival of mediæval notions,—at a time when, as David Riesman says, "Pessimism has become an opiate," and more so than optimism ever was.

IV

AMERICAN NOTES

IF mud-turtles could speak they would sound like my countrymen as I hear them over the radio and in the movies, spreading the mud-turtle language among millions who are led to feel that one ought to speak as if one had mud in the mouth. In this mere viscous noise every syllable is blurred or burred; there is no precision or clarity; no vowel has its value. Well said the novelist Howells, "Who can defend the American accent, which is not so much an accent as a whiffle, a snuffle, a twang?"

*
* *

How generally uniform are American minds.

Percival Lowell, in *Chöson*, speaks of an old Korean map-maker who left America out of his map of the world. But he mentioned some French sailors who were said to have seen it. "On reaching it, they found it to be one vast level wilderness. The only sounds of life which they heard in this great wilderness were the cries of some parrots in the distance."

I seem to remember hearing these cries myself.

*

* *

The so-called Expatriates of the nineteen-twenties made a cult of "living," and they returned in the end to America because this cult is against the American grain. Living as an art was quite unnatural for them. Americans love the ability to do something, as they love power also, far more than they can ever love mere living. A pity, perhaps, but true.

*

* *

The critic Montgomery Schuyler said that *except in architecture* American humour had never found full expression, but he might have added that it had found a fairly full expression in writings *about* American architecture. Schuyler himself referred to certain "disorderly" American modes that called for the intervention of an architectural police, and the architect Louis Sullivan spoke of the "Tubercular" and "Cataleptic" styles which might have been "President Grant" or "Admiral Dewey." Two California crazes were signalized by Bret Harte as the "Union Pacific Renaissance" and the "Comstock Lode" manner, and Ambrose Bierce, in *Can Such Things Be?* described as follows a certain house that was an example of the "Early Comatose" order,—"It appeared to have been designed by an architect who shrank from publicity, and, although unable to conceal his work, did what he honestly could to insure it against a second look."

All these pleasantries recognize that the word "Victorian" is out of place in connection with wooden buildings of a type that Queen Victoria's realm never knew, while they disparage the innumerable fantastic inventions that have served in this country in lieu of a genuine style. What they all seem to say is, We are waiting for the real thing and we will accept no makeshifts in the meantime.

*

* *

Americans are no great shakes at conversation, and one of the reasons for this is that we are too sympathetic. All conversation among sympathetic people tends to adjust itself to the weakest link in the human chain. If one person is self-conscious, they all tend to become self-conscious; if he has a woolly mind the conversation becomes woolly. I have seen a whole

table demoralized by one poor lamb whose secret wish
was merely to be somewhere else.

*

*   *

Whatever their conscious beliefs may be, Americans
are instinctively believers in the freedom of the will.
They may think they are determinists, but, when this
is the case, they always turn out to be fatalists, and
that is quite a different matter. William James made
this clear in his *Principles of Psychology:* "The fatalis-
tic argument is really no argument for simple determinism. There runs through it the sense of a force
which might make things otherwise from one moment
to another, if it were only strong enough to breast the
tide. A person who feels the *impotence* of free effort
in this way has the acutest notion of what is meant
by it, and of its possible independent power. How else
could he be so conscious of its absence and of that of
its effects? But genuine determinism occupies a totally
different ground: not the *impotence* but the *unthink-
ability* of free will is what it affirms."

In this sense, I say that all American fatalism as-
sumes and, as it were, demands free will. It springs
from a kind of disappointment, and this is our char-

acteristic mood from Mark Twain and Henry Adams to Dreiser and Faulkner, whose people are generally defeated, like the people of Hemingway, Dos Passos, Fitzgerald and Farrell. Our world has not lived up to its expectations, and the single man feels helpless before the mass. Hence these tears, or this hard-boiled denial of the right to weep. But this does not argue that free will does not exist; it merely affirms that the will is not effective. It pays the highest tribute to the will, for it says that life is meaningless and empty precisely because of this negation. How many are the Americans, living or dead, for whom the will has not been the core of life, either in its operation or in its suspension?

The only unthinkable thing, for American minds, is that the will should not exist; and that is the reason why, when it is not effective, its impotence seems to Americans so overwhelming. One could never imagine an Asiatic writing as, for instance, Theodore Dreiser wrote. It takes long generations of disappointment, hundreds and thousands of years of disillusion to produce the deterministic frame of mind; or one might more truly say that the real determinist is one who has never known expectations. Fatalism presupposes hope, and any child can be a fatalist. Take away his kite or his train of cars, or lock him up in a closet, and he sees life stretching before him as a prison or a desert. We have lost so many kites, as Henry Adams pointed out, we have had to exchange so many nurseries for closets, that we have ceased to think of ourselves as the children for whom the world was one big vacant lot.

*
* *

"America is an extraordinarily ghostless country." Thus my Irish friend, a lover of ghosts, who compares us with England and his country. He means that America has a great deal of exposed surface, and this is a novelty for Europeans. They are not interested in our nooks and crannies, where the ghosts abound, because these are so much like their own. They come here for new impressions, and our exposed surface gives them a lively, if monotonous, array of these. Our "ghostlessness" is as striking to them as the ghostly is to Americans in Ireland and England, for nothing takes them to Portsmouth or Charleston, for instance, or the pre-urban surroundings of the last generation. But in Vermont, where he spent three years, Kipling found much of the ghostly; and there is no such breeding-ground for ghosts as a rotting old wooden American house in a swamp. What a world Charles Addams has made of these rotting houses! From Hawthorne to Henry James, from Mary E. Wilkins to Faulkner, our story-tellers' world has been peopled with ghosts.

*
*   *

It is the rule that writers flourish best in the oldest part of any country. So New England will never be deserted, nor will the South be. Just so, regionalism flourishes best,—other things being equal,—in the oldest part of the given region.

*
*   *

There have been many attempts to define the dichotomy, as Philip Rahv calls it, between "energy" and "sensibility" in the United States, a contrast or division that he symbolizes in the terms "Redskins" and "Palefaces." But this distinction is literally only skin-deep. The older distinction between "Lowbrow" for energy and "Highbrow" for sensibility still seems to me to express it better, and, even better still perhaps, Theodore Roosevelt's distinction between the Red-bloods and the Mollycoddles. The Red-bloods, or the Redskins,—the party of energy, that is to say,—include Mark Twain, Walt Whitman, Carl Sandburg and so on, while the Mollycoddles or Palefaces—the party of sensibility—include Henry Adams, Henry James and various others. But when one bears down too heavily on metaphors, they are apt to evaporate at once, and one might say that the real distinction resembles the old Russian distinction between the Westernizers and the Slavophiles. For at least an element of these two types is that the Palefaces look towards Europe, just as the Westernizers did in Russia, while the Redskins, like the Slavophiles, are rooted defiantly at home. They are apt to be products of Western, or, one might say, continental experience, as the Palefaces are types of the Eastern seaboard. In general, one type is more important for substance, as the other is more important in style and form; and, while some readers share a taste for both the types in question, one is equally bored when they run too far to extremes.

I would say that the actual parallel which ours resembles most of all is that between the *esprit gaulois* and the *esprit précieux* in France, the two lines that run through all French literature as they run also through our own. Rabelais, Balzac and Dumas, for instance, represent the *esprit gaulois,* just as Mark Twain and Whitman represent it for us, the line of broad humour or native frankness that tends to be careless of literary form and is apt, with us, to run off into what we call hokum. Writers of this type are always aesthetically impure and deficient in literary manners, finesse and taste, but as a rule they excel in human generosity, together with a certain grandeur of imagination. Everyone feels that they cannot be judged by literary standards merely, for they transcend the artistic criteria, adapted to the *esprit précieux,* which are adequate for measuring the nature of this. Meanwhile, as the broad type is apt to run into hokum, the other constantly tends to the opposite abuses. With its distaste for plain people and plain speech, with its devotion to delicacy of phrasing and expression, it is dogged by the pedantries of purism and coldness of heart.

With us these two great types are scarcely on literary speaking terms, while everyone feels that the great thing is the central thing we lack which reconciles the two. In France the *esprit gaulois* and the *esprit précieux* were reconciled by Molière, as everybody knows, —the seventeenth-century playwright who made whole again what history, so to speak, had rent asunder. This great lover of true simplicity, this great hater of the insincere, was on the side of the *esprit gaulois,* mainly, but he had the virtues and sympathies of the *précieux* also. Is it not another Molière that we need here?

*

*   *

How much the state of German literature before the Napoleonic wars resembled the state of American literature before the world-war epoch! Hear what Carlyle said a hundred years ago: "During the greater part of the last century, the Germans, in our intellectual survey of the world, were quietly omitted; a vague contemptuous ignorance prevailed respecting them; it was a Cimmerian land where, if a few sparks did glimmer, it was but so as to testify their own existence, too feebly to enlighten *us*. The Germans passed for apprentices in all provinces of art; and many foreign craftsmen scarcely allowed them so much."

So Americans were regarded only the other day. There was a sounding-board behind European writers that carried their voices across the ocean, while American writers, facing the other way, faced a keen east wind.

*
*   *

Referring to her college days, Elizabeth Shepley Sergeant writes, "American literature had no place in the Bryn Mawr curriculum,—no Melville, no Hawthorne, no Poe, no Dickinson, no Whitman. Henry James and Edith Wharton were the only modern fiction writers; expatriates, you see; and we read them for pleasure, not for study. When, ten years after my graduation, I told one of my English professors that I had discovered a genuine first-class work of American fiction, in which a young woman of prairie background had conceived her world with new eyes and made of it a work of art, she looked at me sceptically. Even *My Ántonia* failed to move her."

How typical that was not only of Bryn Mawr but of Harvard and all our colleges fifty years ago! And equally typical was the frame of mind expressed elsewhere in this writer's memoir of Willa Cather. The passage refers to the revelations in *McClure's Magazine,* of which Willa Cather was managing editor for a while: "A Bryn Mawrster raised by President M. Carey Thomas must try to right these terrible social wrongs that blistered and festered under the shiny urban surface of Manhattan island."

Side by side, these two passages perfectly illustrate Emerson's remark that "we have our culture from one continent and our duties from another,"—which continued to be true up to the first world war.

Time has healed this breach, for Americans no longer look abroad and our eggs are at last all in one basket. But, regarding the future, another question now comes up, Are we going to have any "culture," or any "duties"?

*
* *

What determines the degree of development of a civilization? There is only one criterion, according to
Leopardi,—the amount of the singularity one finds
among the people of the country. To put this in other
words, character exists when people are interested in
it and tolerate it, and variety of character is the life
of civilization.

It is just this variety of character that has largely
passed away with us. There was a time when our
population was full of singularity. In old New England, as in the West and the South, the superior types
were commoner than they are at present, but also, and
this is to be observed, the queer fellows, the odd fish,
the cracker-barrel sages and the like,—the village
atheists, even the town drunkards,—had a sort of
privilege, as they had in Russia. They might have
been considered reprobates, but they were encouraged
as amusing, if not worthy of respect; people seemed to
realize that some of them were geniuses, *in posse* if not
in esse. Towards all such persons, in recent times, the
general attitude is one of impatience, and they have
almost died out with the Shakers and other sects that
once gave such variety to the human landscape. This

indicates, if we are to believe Leopardi, a definite retrogression in our civilization.

I think, for instance, of the old Shaker museum at Harvard village. There one finds the manuscript books that were copied by the brothers, as the monks copied manuscripts in the Middle Ages. This native American monastic life, devoted to weaving, wood-carving and so on, is only one of the old life-patterns of which we have lost all memory. A century and a half ago, the popular mind was filled with examples from the Bible, and men like Josiah Smith, Elias Hicks and Lorenzo Dow lived out, in the fullest modern daylight, a dream-life drawn from the world of the ancient Jews. During every moment of their westward trek, the Mormons followed in imagination the exodus of Moses and his people from their land of bondage. Just so, the unkempt Lorenzo Dow, emerging in some forest settlement, acted the role of Elijah, with his camel-skin coat, appearing with his words of warning at the gates of a city. Others dreamed of the Essenes or of John the Baptist, while John Brown, on his errands of the Lord, as he supposed they were, thought no more of the shedding of blood than the God-intoxicated heroes he had found in the Bible.

Along with these biblical models, the popular mind was filled with the models presented by Cicero and

Plutarch, so that all the classical modes of living were latent in the general imagination. They had only to be touched into action by inspired leaders. It was this preliminary work accomplished by popular custom that made possible the influence of Jefferson, or of Garrison, or Thoreau.

What followed was that "strange unloosen'd wondrous time" that Whitman mentioned,—I think in *Specimen Days*,—the time that Lafcadio Hearn contrasted in a letter with the stratified, solidified America that he knew later. "How much better seems," he said, "the wild days of Mormon evangelization,—of the free-love phalansteries, of Brook Farm and the Oneida community, of Hepworth Dixon's 'spiritual wives'! Humbug, of course, but what a finely fluid aspirational condition of society the whole thing meant, —even with 'Mr. Sludge, the medium' thrown in!"

Among the relics of our older time, how real were these life-patterns and this condition that have passed utterly out of the memory of men.

*

* *

How explain the fact, so strange to Europeans, that Americans regard expatriation as a kind of treason? It is because they are born parts of a still unformed organism, and their American instinct requires them to share in the forming of this organism. As a rule, they feel this organic political need. It is the recognition of their societal instinct in the peculiar circumstances to which they are born; and this leads them to feel that those who do not share it are somehow traitors. Is this not why they are so often uneasy if they remain for a long time abroad?

It is because America is still unformed that Americans tend to be overborne in Europe, paying an exaggerated tribute to the form of others. Here lies the grain of truth in D. H. Lawrence's statement that America is a "spirit-homeland," not yet a "blood-homeland." Americans of the more recent stocks have scarcely any roots here and the pioneer habit of shifting bases has prevented even the oldest stocks from putting down deep roots in large parts of the country. How, under these conditions, could they have acquired a blood-homeland here,—and does not any sort of transplantation condemn them still further to a surface existence? This explains for me the general feeling that Archibald MacLeish sums up in his *American Letter*,—

> Here we must eat our salt or our bones starve.
> Here we must live or live only as shadows.

It seems odd, at first sight, that the great "Slavophile" Dostoievsky shared, for his country, this typically

American feeling. During his years of forced expatriation, he was morbidly afraid of losing touch with Russia. In Dresden, Geneva, Florence and Milan, he felt "like a slice cut from a loaf," saying that he could not live without Russia, that he could not write without Russia and that to "get out of touch with Russia" was to lose the power to write. Dostoievsky's daughter, in her biography, remarked that Turgenev spent his whole life abroad and "remained eternally Russian," while her father's "Russianism" depended, as he always felt, on his bodily presence in Russia. Why was this? It was because he was only partly of Russian blood, his daughter said, because he was a "Lithuanian," a "Norman," a "German," and therefore felt he was in danger of being "absorbed by Europe." There we see the same causes at work that produce in American minds the same effect.

It strikes me that André Gide summed the question up in writing about Maurice Barrès's book *Les Déracinés*. Barrès had advised French writers not to uproot themselves but to stay at home in their provincial surroundings, and Gide remarked that Barrès had only been able to write the book because he had failed to follow his own counsel. For could he have written so eloquently if he had not uprooted himself, if he had not left the provinces and gone to Paris? But, as

Gide said, Barrès was strong, and transplantation is good for the strong,—"This is the education that the strong demand." As for the weak, on the other hand,—how about them? *"Quant aux faibles,"*—Gide said,—*"enracinez, enracinez!*—the weak should root themselves, they should root themselves." In this sense, Americans are, in countless cases, weak,—which further explains their instinctive feeling that they should stay at home.

V

THE LITERARY LIFE

THE great question for a writer is to find his focus, and to keep himself focussed. When he is out of focus he is in hell.

*
* *

When a writer begins to be successful, when he begins to soar, outwardly but especially inwardly, then, to save him from infatuation, he needs to be pelted with bitter apples.

*
* *

Nothing good can come from writers who are at ease in their Zion. We should all live like Israelites at the Feast of Passover.

*
* *

"I have always noticed," said Boileau, returning from Versailles after one of his audiences with Louis XIV, "that when the conversation did not turn on his praise the King was bored and ready to go away." Sainte-Beuve, quoting this in his essay on Madame Récamier, adds, "Every great poet when growing old is on that point a little like Louis XIV," a fact that I have verified in the presence of two poets who have at least some claim to be described as great. I have noted that their opinion of other writers, especially critics, is almost entirely determined by what these writers have said, or thought, or done with reference to *them*, and that, if not vain, they were deeply egotistical and became all the more so as they advanced in life.

This ever-increasing egotism of the literary mind is a sort of occupational or vocational disease, and it springs from the fact that their own personalities are the stock-in-trade of writers, for their work is literally spun from the "ego and his own." Subjectivity and isolation are their governing conditions. It is natural enough that, in many cases, from over-cultivation, their egos are as morbid as the liver of a Strasbourg goose.

This explains why many poets,—and other writers,—are never happy unless incense is perpetually swung before them, for their self-esteem grows tenderer every day; and it also explains why even the greatest cannot forgive persistently hostile reviewers. For, since they and their work are virtually identical, they feel that attacks on their writing are attacks on themselves. To what a sorry pass of low spirits and ill health reviewers have been known to bring writers of genius, even to the point of killing them, as Shelley said of Keats,— sometimes because their work is their only compensation for a general sense of ineptitude and failure in life.

*

* *

Some people are born free, but most people have to win their freedom. They are obliged to work to win it, as they have to work to keep up their tone. There are those who win it through the constant habit of a focussed mind that is always overcoming a certain resistance, while others do it by risking their lives in one way or another, in dangerous sports, for instance, or in big-game hunting. Lucky are those who, having an aim, can keep their wits in motion to realize it.

Aldous Huxley somewhere says that he becomes ill when he does not work, when he ceases to work even for two or three days, and the author of the *Portrait of Barrie* remarks that this author "came alive the moment he began to work again. He would look kindled, brisk, alert, his very step became resolute, almost jaunty," when he had undergone "the lovely experience—the slinging of sheet after sheet onto the floor." On the other hand, when the idea of a play turned out not to be feasible, "I could see the light go out in his saddening eyes."

Lafcadio Hearn once wrote, "You say I work well. If I did not, I should go insane or become a prey to nervous disease." This,—and its corollary also,—is true of most writers. I remember Joseph Conrad's description of his first glimpse of Stephen Crane, who rode out to meet this admirer at the gate of his house, looking as ever at his best on horseback, "with the confident bearing of a man who is feeling very sure of the present and the future." According to Conrad, this was "all because he was looking at life from the saddle with a good morning's work behind him. Nothing more is needed to give a man a blessed moment of illusion." I once saw William Faulkner in this state of mind, striding along, with his legs thrown out, on Madison Avenue in New York, as if he were the sole proprietor of all creation.

Take away this gift and power and a writer can seem utterly crushed, like an addict who is unable to obtain his drug. I saw this in the case of one of the most famous and brilliant of novelists whom everybody read in the last generation. He had carried all before him with his romantic charm, and then at the last he was a shadow of himself, uneasy, suspicious, frightened, weak and grey. It was true he had given up drinking and lost the illusions that alcohol gives; but what he had mainly lost was the life-line of his talent. This is the horrid possibility that haunts many writers.

*

* *

A cellar on a rainy day is good for writing. I have found that a rainy day in Florida,—and in California also,—wonderfully prospers the act of mental concentration. That is one reason why England, Ireland and Norway are so good for writers.

I have always felt that the sunshine in California has an ill effect on people's minds there. My friend M.W. gave me a case in point. The superior of the Roman Catholic seminary at San Mateo complained that he could not get his students to work. Impossible to induce a vocation! The students were always sitting about in the sun. That is why the Spaniards and Italians who have lived in these warm sunny climates and who have cared greatly for the inner life, have cultivated gloomy depths of darkness. They have known how to adjust themselves to this semi-tropical milieu. They have broken up the monotony of heat and sunshine by creating contrasts,—high and heavy walls, damp stonework, enclosures of deep shade, thickets of shrubbery and so on. Not California bungalows or Florida verandahs but bare stony walls, houses like Michelangelo's at Florence,—these assist the mind to find its focus.

In short, a dwelling without penetralia,—the "inner chambers" of the Roman house,—is anything but favourable to the life of the mind; and is that not something to consider when one thinks of Frank Lloyd Wright, the greatest architectural genius of our epoch? This extraordinary man is an architect for extroverts, and what would become of the thinking and the feeling types if, beyond a point, he had his way? He is an expression of the epoch of *The Lonely Crowd*, when the "inner-directed" mind has given place to the "other-directed" who have nothing to lose by living in beautiful fish-bowls.

*

* *

The Artful Dodger. Get the reputation of being a recluse. Spread it about that you are a chronic invalid. Tell them you have leprosy or rabies. You must be

> instinctively thorough
> About your crevice and burrow,

like Robert Frost's Drumlin Woodchuck.

*
* *

Why is "good society," or so much of it, insupportable,
in spite of its charm of good manners, courage and
grace? Because it consists so largely of powerful un-
enlightened people who see life in terms of ceremonial
and their own importance. They hear and they consider only what they wish to hear, only what conduces
to their own comfort, thinking what one wishes to
think instead of what one *has* to think, however dis-
concerting the truth may be. They rationalize everything until it fits their pattern. But thinking what one
has to think is thinking in terms of real values, and
this alone is endurable to people with minds.

What else did Ruskin mean when he said that "an
artist should be fit for the best society and keep out of
it"? In America, at least, as Edith Wharton pointed
out, writers and artists have usually fled from the
world of fashion. (Not that this hostility has been
one-sided. Mrs. Winthrop Chanler said that "the
Four Hundred would have fled in a body from a poet,
a painter, a musician or a clever Frenchman.") And
was this not so even in England when the world of
intellect had something in common with the world
of fashion? Hazlitt said that those who are accustomed
to the talk of literary men cannot put up with any

other and that "persons in high life talk almost entirely by rote and have no opinions but what will
please. Beside the conversation of authors, the conversation of men of fashion is flat, insipid, stale and
unprofitable." Hazlitt continues, "They talk about
much the same things,—pictures, poetry, politics, plays,
but they do it worse and at a sort of vapid second-
hand. They, in fact, talk out of newspapers and magazines *what we write there.* They do not feel the same
interest in the subjects they affect to handle with an
air of fashionable condescension . . . Were it not for
the wine and the dessert," Hazlitt concludes, "no
author in his senses would accept an invitation to a
well-dressed dinner-party, except out of pure good
nature and unwillingness to disoblige by his refusal."
All of which might have been said a hundred years
later.

> Not here, O Apollo,
> Are haunts meet for thee.

*

* *

People who are too agreeable and cultivated lull
one insensibly into a kind of fatuity. One gets into a
fool's paradise. That is another reason why, except
in small doses, "good society,"—at its best,—is not good

for writers. For the literary mind needs to be misunderstood; it requires something harsh in the air that surrounds it.

Children and writers feel the need of grit and sand, of something astringent in the moral atmosphere, that causes them to define themselves and their aims, as one needs salt in one's diet, as the teeth require both alkali and acids.

As much as to understanding, children are entitled to misunderstanding. Not the brutal variety, but the bland variety. After the primitive needs have received attention, they should be confronted with a blank wall of incomprehension. It is by reacting against this that they define themselves, become aware of themselves and their intentions.

The same thing is true of writers and artists, and this is one reason why England has been so fertile in geniuses. The stolid egoism of the English household is the milieu for poets. Americans are too sympathetic to provide a good milieu for the development of individuality. They are always talking about and trying to meet its problems, and by this very process they inhibit its growth. The process merely produces self-conscious hobbledehoys. Everyone, in fact, needs incomprehension, and even oceans of it; and this is especially true of writers and artists. It is usually because we are misunderstood by others that we come to understand ourselves.

The infallible way to produce uniformity is to cultivate individuality, which, in its proper growth, is always a by-product. The great age of American genius, just before the Civil War,—certainly not yet equalled in this respect by any succeeding generation,—was an age of rigid social discipline. Michelet said that he grew up like a blade of grass between two paving-stones. So did Thoreau, Emerson and Hawthorne. So did Emily Dickinson and Winslow Homer. It is true that Poe and Melville encountered too much incomprehension. The last straw breaks the camel's back, but at least a certain proportion of the other straws serve to develop its muscles.

*
* *

Today I received another of those questionnaires that are so often sent out to writers, asking for my views on public questions and "how the American author ought to stand" regarding this, that and the other matter. I fully agree that writers should "take sides," and I always do so; but I ignore or decline these invitations to develop my views at length. It is not that

I have not strong feelings on many of these subjects;
but may heaven preserve me from expressing them
beyond the point of a Yes or No until the spirit calls
me to do so in the normal course of my writing. Well
said Nietzsche, "How happy are we, we finders of
knowledge, provided that we know how to keep silent
long enough." If there is anything "the American
author ought" to do, it is to keep the steam in his own
boiler. If, storing away their opinions, writers allowed
them to roll up interest in their minds, their legitimate
writings would have a weight which they generally
lack at present.

*

* *

I sympathize with my youthful neighbour who is
struggling to inject a little order, a little taste and style,
—a little readability, in short,—into a mass of manuscript that is supposed to be a book. A great lawyer
thinks he has written this book, and he proposes to
sign it. These legal luminaries, these magnates, these
presidents of corporations, these very important men
who are always pressing buttons have notions of their
own in regard to writing. They imagine that all they
have to do, to commit their thoughts to immortality,
is to command a squadron of secretaries to look this,

that and the other up, and then, in some hour of
ease, with their spoils assembled about them, and a
box of the best cigars on the desk before them, dictate
to Miss Daphne or Miss Hebe. And they are always
surprised to find that no one will read their writings.
So many *whereases* and *wherefores* have crept into
their manuscript that, although Miss Hebe strives to
conceal the fact, she would rather walk home to River-
side Drive in a March blizzard than read a page of
the great man's lucubrations. Then the same result
always follows. The great man turns for help to some
youthful writer and offers him a chauffeur's wages
if he will take the manuscript in hand and make it
worthy of his signature.

These important men do not know that writing is
a learned profession, much more difficult than law.
They do not know that some problems cannot be
solved by pressing a button, that literary taste and
skill are the reward of years of humble effort. And
in this they resemble certain writers who are also important, if one judges them by a similar standard, their
income and the decorations they have received. One
knows of authors who hire young men and women to
do their drudgery for them. But God is not mocked
in regard to them, nor is the critic deceived. This was
not the way that Gibbon worked, or Prescott or Park-

man, who used the secretarial crutch only because they were halt and blind. A real writer feels about his work as a healthy mother feels about her baby. His instinct revolts against the incubator and every mechanical substitute for brooding. The writer who does not brood, in every sense of the word, the writer who is not his own drudge, who does not earn his notes by loving investigation, pays a heavy forfeit. His prose lacks flavour, tone and texture, and nothing can compensate for this.

I add that no good writer has ever liked drudgery, and Prescott and Parkman, for instance, found research repulsive. The tension created by this repulsion is characteristic of first-rate minds. *— this certainly denigrates research.*

* *

I never get anything out of abstract discussions. They never rouse my mind. Whatever they might give, I get from a novel of Balzac better. A good novel at once heats my mind and sets the source of all my perceptions flowing. A Balzac "interior" recalls my interiors; his *ville de province,* my own; his types, my types,— and all the bells begin to ring in my buried city.

*

* *

How to dispose of one's rubbish. When one is living perhaps in the woods and writing in the morning, this is the sort of problem that provides one's afternoons with a proper focus.

Bertrand Russell is right in saying that one who wishes to do good work must expect to be bored much of the time. A state of dull vacuity is the best mental state in which to suspend one's hours of composition. When the conscious mind is over-stimulated, the unconscious mind refuses to open its door. So, at least, it is with me.

"The fierce and callous egotism of the artist comes to its perfection in a vast expanse of custom, leisure and apparently vacuous reverie." So said Arnold Bennett, who added that, because of this, most English writers live in the country. I noticed, reading Emerson's Journal, that, when he was at St. Augustine, he spent hours along the beach driving an orange with his walking-stick. Day after day, at St. Augustine, when I was writing well there, my only object was to find another coquina shell, washed up by the tide, to take home and use for baking fish in.

VI

ON WORDS

THE Irish poet James Stephens said that the trouble with American writers is, quite simply, that "they don't love words." I think there is some truth in this and I wonder if the reason is that, in the matter of words, we are so "scientific." How could we share, if we wished it, the fine careless rapture of the poets of pre-scientific times? For them words were laden with associations that we, with our semantics, are driven to reject.

A Swiss professor says that "a kind of language consciousness appears to be more generally developed in America than elsewhere," leading to an extreme awareness of the "errors of verbal suggestion" and the misunderstandings caused by "verbal trappings." But how can any intense whole-hearted love of words survive this constant verbal scepticism? The love of words springs out of the unconscious. It comes from a long devotion to the language one inherits, and it cannot abide attempts to create new kinds of language or a too conscious scrutiny of the old kinds.

*
*   *

David Riesman has one of those minds that set one's own mind racing. In his field no writer since Veblen has been so exciting. But he is one of the writers who "don't love words," and sad indeed, in his case, are the consequences. His three great categories, "tradition-directed," "inner-directed" and "other-directed," have opened an era in sociological thinking, but two of these phrases are ungrammatical, unless I am mistaken, and barbarous from a rhetorical point of view. And what unhappy metaphors he constantly uses!— "overlaid with swings of fashion," "harnessed to the same mobility drives" and "energies channelled by the rich into their leisure budget." For what purpose do we pursue the study of language when our most perceptive minds abound in this jargon?

*
*   *

Sherwood Anderson always said that Gertrude Stein made words "fresh," while Leo Stein said that for him words never grew stale, adding, "Words competently used seem to me as effective as ever." Sherwood Anderson's feeling was entirely sincere, but would he have felt this so strongly if he had not been an adver-

tising man who had spent much of his life in a journalistic world? The prevalence of journalism in our
time, especially with Americans, so many of whom
have also been advertising writers, unaware of the
resources of English and used to verbal counterfeiting,
accounts in part for the vogue of Gertrude Stein.

*

* *

Willa Cather's favourite word was "splendour," or so
says her friend Elizabeth Shepley Sergeant. It was a
word that "recurred so often in her talk, her books, and
the letters of those years, that I think of her as living
it out."

In many writers we find this sort of key-word that
indicates some central tendency in their organization.
Thus, for example, "significant," Goethe's favourite
word, was certainly indicative in this fashion, and so
is the word "renewal," which occurs early and late,
constantly, in the writings of Lewis Mumford. The
word alone explains for me why I am drawn to this
writer, with his ever-renewed sense of the possibilities
of life. Similarly, in Edith Wharton, one repeatedly
finds the word "throne," or "throned," indicating her
taste for the regal posture, as "manly" was Parkman's
favourite word, "purple" was Edgar Saltus's and

"doom" and "fate" are William Faulkner's. So Jack London's key-word was "wolf." He sometimes signed his letters "The Wolf," he called his house "Wolf House," one of his best-drawn characters was Wolf Larsen, and he told his own story symbolically in the story of the Alaska dog that reverted to the wolf-pack in order to survive. He saw his own cult of Nietzsche as the cult of the wolf. In just this way, "hawk" is Robinson Jeffers's key-word. The writer of "Give your heart to the hawks" called the tower he built "Hawk Tower," and the bird of prey that soared over it symbolized his expressed belief that violence is "the sire of all the world's values."

In how many other cases does one word sum up the central feeling of the man within the writer.

*

* *

It is a long time since I have seen the word "imponderable" used as a noun in the liberal weeklies, but there was a day when no issue of *The Nation* or *The New Republic* could have been described as complete without it. One was always reading of the "imponderables" of this and that, and I remember when and how it first appeared, when it dawned as it were in the mind of liberal circles. The word was Bismarck's,—it was a favourite word of his,—and Harold Laski quoted it in a review in *The Nation*. After that, for several years, scarcely a fortnight went by without one's hearing of "the imponderables, as Bismarck called them."

How many of these phrases,—"Ripeness is all," "It is later than you think,"—resound for a season and then are heard no more. They wear out their welcome in the end, like the phrase "a dim view," and as fireworks sparkle for a moment to be suddenly extinguished. One of the longest to survive has been "No man is an island." John Donne uttered it and T. S. Eliot popularized it when he rehabilitated Donne, and it is surely unlikely that Hemingway would have unearthed it himself if Donne's writings had not already been above ground. But when it became the motto of *For Whom the Bell Tolls* it passed with lightning speed into the public domain, and instantly new editions of Donne were published and disposed of and booksellers were obliged to report that they were "out of Donne." One could not keep up with the rage and the phrase itself became over-night a cliché of advertising. "No man is an island" was soon as familiar as *E Pluribus Unum,* Virgil's ancient phrase for a salad dressing.

*

* *

There is, of course, an American language, and
Mencken records it very well, but I wonder how far
this language has conquered the literary mind of the
country and how far it will ever conquer this. How
far has even Mencken used it? Never, at least, in his
"serious" writing, as Albert Jay Nock pointed out
years ago, remarking that his *Treatise on Right and
Wrong* might, so far as the language went, have been
written by Bishop Butler of the *Analogy of Religion*.
I can scarcely see how his books on the American language itself would have been different if they had
been written in England. Nor can I see any trace of
the American language in Thornton Wilder, for instance, or Katherine Anne Porter, any more than in
Ellen Glasgow or Willa Cather. When novelists record the conversation of "drug-store Romeos," they
have no choice but to use the American language; but
otherwise Mencken's great work seems to me like the
Kinsey reports, which record another phase of reality perhaps equally well. For when one has said this,
one is obliged to add that neither Kinsey nor Mencken
excels as a guide to conduct. If one draws from them
the inference, "Everybody is doing it,—therefore, go
thou and do likewise," one is inferring, in Mencken's
case, what good writers do not do, and I doubt very
much if they will ever do it.

Why this is so,—if I am right,—Mencken himself explained in his lively essay on Ring Lardner, who was a very good writer in a limited sense,—one might call him a two-dimensional writer. He "handled magnificently," as Mencken said, the "American vulgate," but Mencken went on to describe this as a "dialect" and, what is more, a dialect that "will pass"; and no serious writer wants to use a language that is not stable and permanent, that will not last. He does not want to use a language that is going to "turn black" like the badly mixed pigments of some of our old painters, a language made up of words that are good for this year only and will soon seem as flat as the slang of a dozen years ago. There was truth in Vachel Lindsay's remark, in a published letter to one of his friends, "John V. A. Weaver seems to be the hero of Mencken's big book." This was the Weaver who wrote *In American* thirty years ago and whose writing can scarcely be said to have worn very well.

*

* *

It is certain that much English usage, and some of the strongest, simplest and best, has passed out of our consciousness altogether. When one sees on an English road "Dead slow. Please hoot," or, in a library, "Tread

lightly and speak little," one feels how much, in this
matter, we Americans have lost. Still, I think that at
present American writers are more prone to use Oxford dictionaries than either Mencken or Webster.
(And, according to one biographer, Fowler's *Modern
English Usage* is President Eisenhower's Bible in literary matters.) In this respect they carry on the habit
of the old New England authors who invariably preferred to Webster, the Americanizer, the traditional
Worcester's dictionary that preserved the overtones
and flavours of words, the poetic element in words
that writers like. For the rest, I have always been
sceptical of attempts to see an "American rhythm,"
along with an American language, in American writers, aside from the few, good writers and bad alike,
in whom these tendencies obviously do exist. I remember that, in the "free verse" days, Mary Austin prophesied that all American poetry would assume this form
because she had seen in it a natural American Indian
form, and what the Indians were we were destined
to become. She went on at great length about the
American rhythm that corresponded with the movement of the red men through the forest,—and I think
the westward tramping of the pioneers,—but, far from
becoming the predestined rhythm of American poets,
"free verse" itself vanished in a dozen years.

*
* *

What is becoming of the useful and harmless adverb *well*? "I'm pretty *good* off" and "I can't see you *good*" are established phrases in American fiction now that Hemingway and Faulkner so often use them. A supposedly educated man in Faulkner's *The Wild Palms* says, "I shaved this morning but not good," a usage that is so far the rule in Hemingway's interviews, at least, that readers have almost ceased to notice it.

How much in this way is the American language mere disintegrated English? It does not make me happy to hear that a professor has been driven to write, and is able to write, a book called *Who Killed Grammar*? In this he speaks of the "anything goes" school of teaching, and I agree with him that "the world-wide use of English imposes obligations on teachers." But how far can teachers prevail in the end when they are opposed by the two most famous living novelists?

I remember a phrase of the painter John Sloan, "Any man who speaks English with care is suspected of being a fairy nowadays." But is this a good reason for pretending that one has no education?

*
* *

One may well object to people who are "tired of grammar," like the lady in the story of Henry B. Fuller, but much can be said for those who are innocent of it.

I asked Mrs. D., a country neighbour, if she would take in as a lodger one of my friends. She replied in the following words that she could not do so: "I won't have nobody snoopin' round my house, not for no price."

The splendour of this fourfold negative might lead one to regret that grammar was ever invented.

*
* *

Our standard authors are quite inconsistent in the matter of spelling. In *The Scarlet Letter*,—the second edition, which I have, and which was presumably proof-read by Hawthorne himself, perhaps at the post-office, as his custom was,—I find on a single page "neighbour" spelled with a *u* and "honored" spelled without it. Elsewhere in the same book "colored" and "favored" are spelled as I write them, while "demeanour" has the *u*. Howells's novels are inconsistent in the same way, as if, between "English" and "American" spelling, this writer could never make up his mind. Thus, so far as good usage goes, the question remains optional. But I notice that, among our best modern writers, Robert Frost is only one of many who, more or less consistently, use "English" spelling.

Not to go into the subsoil motives for all this, I prefer "English" spelling for a very good reason. Everyone writes "glamour" even now, because the *u* is so obviously part of the glamour. But the word "honour" has glamour also. All good words have glamour for me.

*

* *

No one should ever publish a book until he has read it aloud to a woman. A letter from Madame Roland, written about 1790, gives me a good reason for thinking this. "Do you know," she asks, "that Massachusetts is a very barbarous name? And that a man of fashion was never known to utter such a word when saying soft things to the fair sex? I have heard of a lady who was so shocked at the sound of Transylvania, which was quite new to her, that she desired the impertinent speaker to leave the room."

I protest on behalf of Massachusetts, but the principle stands. (And even regarding Massachusetts the French still have their rights. Léon Bazalgette, who said he could not endure this word, but who was obliged to use it, called it "le Mass.") Women are the arbiters of words, and we should listen to them because they live close to the meanings of words. Men become infatuated with words in and for themselves. Women are closer to the general life, the source of good style, while men tend to live the specialized life, the source of bad style. So women will never allow one to say "obfuscate" when "bewilder" will do just as well; and they shiver at words like "historicity" and will not be comforted if we use them.

VII

NOTES ON NOVELISTS

Our age of psychology is not an age of interest in human nature. Think of the excited wonder with which the novels of Dickens and Balzac were written, a wonder that vibrates in their pages. Theirs was also the day of the great portrait-painters, when Ingres was still living and Sir Thomas Lawrence was not long dead and when competent successors of Gilbert Stuart were affirming in this country that character was absorbingly interesting and wonderfully real.

Good as our novels and portraits may be, they lack this relish for character which has stamped all the enduring novels and portraits. Our novelists turn their characters inside out and sometimes describe them inimitably, but can one imagine a writer of our time laughing and weeping over his characters, living their lives and sharing their feelings as Victor Hugo, for instance, did? When Thackeray said of his characters, "I know the sound of their voices," and Balzac, refusing to talk about ordinary people, said, "Let's get on to the real ones," meaning his own, they were saying what Anthony Trollope said in his autobiography about his "moving, living human creatures . . . I have wandered alone among the rocks and woods, crying at their grief, laughing at their absurdities and thoroughly enjoying their joy. When I shall feel that this intimacy ceases, then I shall know that the old horse should be turned out to grass."

*

*   *

This excited wonder over human nature was one of the marks of the Victorian age, as of all the ages of energy. Is there a portrait-photographer living who has an eye for character that is comparable to David Octavius Hill's? Stieglitz had an eye for certain types, but he was more interested in other matters. The aim and the effect of our portrait-photographers is to make their sitters conform to a preconceived type, captains of industry or pretty women, when they are not decorative arrangements. Well spoke Emerson, writing to Carlyle about his "thirsty eyes," his "portrait-eating, portrait-painting eyes." All the great older novelists and portrait-painters have "eaten" their characters in this way.

Psychology has atomized and split the old idea of character, for which certain modern novelists do not pretend to care. Thus D. H. Lawrence once wrote: "You mustn't look in my novel for the old stable ego of the character . . . Somehow, that which is physic —non-human—in humanity is more interesting to me than the old-fashioned human element, which causes one to conceive a character in a certain moral scheme and make him consistent." Aldous Huxley comments on this, "For ordinary practical purposes we conceive of human beings as creatures with characters. But analysis of their behaviour can be carried so far that they cease to have character and reveal themselves as collections of psychological atoms." The elements that make up a tree interest some people more than the tree itself, but for most people it is the tree that matters; and it is the "old-fashioned human element" for which we look in novels and, owing largely to Freud, seldom find.

*
* *

Along with Freud's analysis, there is another reason for this great change in novels and portraits. In his *Origins of Modern Sculpture*, W. R. Valentiner observes that modern portraits are less good than the old ones because the age of individualism has come to an end. There is small regard, in a collectivist epoch, for personal singularity, a fact that led Ezra Pound to ask whether "we can concede such emphasis to the individual elegy and to personal sadness." Pound was referring to Thomas Hardy's poems, and in line with this he bade farewell to the "doddard" Palgrave and his all too personal *Golden Treasury* of poems.

Psychology and collectivism have thus gone hand in hand in destroying the old feeling for character and human nature. Psychology is one thing,—it is the dominant thing today; and have not the Germans, who invented psychology, shown how remote it is from perception and feeling? That they know less about human nature than other Europeans is the conclusion of many after two world wars. Did any people ever make so many bad guesses about the motives, the behaviour and the character of others?

*

* *

"The only thing I care for in history is the anecdotes." Thus Prosper Mérimée wrote in a great age of the novel, and the decay of the interest in character that marks the modern novel is accompanied by a contempt for anecdotes. It used to be said in the days when Cézanne first became widely known that he had abolished the anecdote in painting, and this word soon

became a byword in literature also. Nowadays all anecdotes, whether they are told for their own sake or to
illustrate character, are anathema to critics. Times
have changed since Edward Lear consoled himself
during a dull winter in France reading nine volumes
of Horace Walpole's letters and the eight volumes of
the memoirs of Thomas Moore, virtually all consist-
ing of anecdotes merely; times have changed since the
days when John Adams found the memoirs of Grimm,
the old French gossip, "the most entertaining book I
ever read." Thomas Jefferson, thinking of Grimm,
whom he had known in Paris, longed for a similar
work by an American hand. Fifteen volumes of anecdotes, within the compass of his own time, written, as
he said, by a man of taste, would have turned back
the clock for him in favour of life.

*

* *

If the present scorn of anecdotes meant merely a
hatred of chitchat, one might feel it was only a symp-
tom of the pressure of the times. In days like ours the
inessential must go to the wall. But there was nothing
trivial in the minds of Jefferson and Adams,—they
were profoundly interested in the characters of men;
and the contempt for the anecdote that one sees in

criticism nowadays is part of the indifference to character of which I have spoken. The critical movement that diverts attention from the "poet" to the "poetry," —the movement that gave rise to a new critical epoch, —incidentally illustrates a larger tendency of the time that has been called the "dehumanization of art." The idea spread through the literary world that, as Allen Tate puts it, "personality" cannot "give up the key to anyone's verse," though this might lead one to ask why Johnson ever wrote lives of the poets or why literary biography has ever legitimately thriven. It has thriven, as a matter of fact, because the lives of authors *do* give up, largely, the key to their verse and their prose by explaining the origins and growth of their tendencies and "vision," what their work "means" and what it "says,"—though of course this does not interest minds that care only for structures and textures, without regard to meanings or character either. The dehumanization in question is symptomatic of a time that has witnessed the virtual extinction of portrait-painting, a time in which "*you* no longer count," as one of the war novels put it, and "private stars fade . . . where two worlds strive."

*

* *

Among critics, F. R. Leavis scouts the idea of creating in fiction "characters that go on living outside the book," and whenever we think of a recent novelist who has conspicuously created these we realize that he belongs to an old-fashioned type. Sinclair Lewis, for one example, created a dozen characters, from Babbitt to Cass Timberlane, Gottlieb, Arrowsmith and Dodsworth, but did this count for anything in the minds of critics? They were only concerned, towards the end of his life, with technical questions of dialogue and pace, flash-backs, the presence of violence in a novel and what not. All this bears out Ortega's remark that, in every department of art, "flight from the human person" is a note of the epoch, as even a "real loathing of living forms of living beings" is characteristic of modern painting and sculpture. The dehumanization of art, for Ortega, implied that, to the modern mind, art itself was "of no transcendent importance" but rather a form of "play and nothing else," and, while he found this feeling sympathetic, he said that the novel was "moribund" in consequence of it.

When, later, Ortega wrote *Notes on the Novel*, hoping the novel might survive and grow, he said there was only one thing that could make this possible,—the "invention of interesting characters." But does this not imply a *re*humanization of art that will bring about a revival of the anecdote also?

*
* *

In expounding his doctrine that "the novel" is to be judged by its "oneness," Henry James said that Tolstoy and Balzac could never have followed his method: "The promiscuous shiftings of standpoint and centre of Tolstoy and Balzac, for instance . . . are the inevitable result of the quantity of presenting their genius launches them in . . . With the complexity they pile up they *can* get no clearness without trying again and again for new centres." (Letter to Mrs. Humphry Ward, 1899.)

But does this not invalidate the *general* authority of James's writings on the art of fiction? Does it not show that James's theories are good for Jamesian novels only, or novels of a similar tenuity and paucity of subject-matter?

Is there, moreover, any such thing as "the" novel,— that notion of many critics nowadays? Is there one peculiar form that constitutes the ideal novel, the laws of which have been gradually revealed, so that the perfect novel can at last be written? Or are there not rather countless types of possible novels, as numerous and as various as the minds that write them?

Surely, on this subject D. H. Lawrence uttered the last word when he remarked to one of his friends: "Tell Arnold Bennett that all rules of construction hold good only for novels which are copies of other novels. A book which is not a copy of other books has its own construction, and what he calls faults, he being an old imitator, I call characteristics."

What Kipling said of poems is true of novels also: "There are nine and sixty ways of constructing tribal lays, and every single one of them is right." So it is also with novels.

*

*   *

George Gissing was one of the writers who thrive on their irritations. "Every man," he says somewhere, "has his intellectual desire; mine is to escape life as I know it, and dream myself back into that old world," the Mediterranean world of the past that gave him a scale by which to measure the scenes that surrounded him in London; and in the last years of his life he set out to seek the traces of it in the Magna Græcia of which he wrote in *By the Ionian Sea*. What was it then that kept him for so many years confined in his City of Dreadful Night?—for he felt about London much as James Thomson felt. Not poverty alone. He hated London with all the instincts of the born recluse. He was offended by crowds, he shrank from casual encounters, he disliked the "tongue of Whitechapel" and the "blaring lust of life." "Every day," he said, "gives me a deeper loathing of city life. If I cannot escape from it to die among green fields, my end will be wretched indeed." Yet virtually his whole life was passed in cities, and, of his twenty-two novels, twenty-one deal, at least largely, with London. In short, his instinct of artistic self-preservation was at war with all his normal tastes.

Is it not a fact that novelists usually thrive on their irritations? Hawthorne's mind throve in the dust and wind of Salem. Flaubert, Stendhal, Sinclair Lewis, Dreiser are other cases in point. As Renan said, "Well being produces only inertia. Discomfort is the principle of movement." Perhaps the less we satisfy our tastes, the more they serve to give us a scale and a measure.

One might sum up the question in Lessing's remark about the town of Brunswick: "It is not that I do not like Brunswick, but that nothing good comes of being long in a place one likes."

*

* *

In one of his letters, Melville praised what he called "oldageifying youth in books," as one of the two great arts that were yet to be discovered, and he tried in *Redburn* to extract and reproduce the antiquated style of an obsolete Liverpool guide-book. The seventeenth-century flavour of many a page of *Moby Dick* was the fruit of a taste as consciously cherished and developed as the taste of certain American painters from William Page to Duveneck for the so-called "brown sauce" of the school of Munich. These painters also wished to achieve the amber patina of age, the sombre harmonious richness of so many old masters, attempting to reach this normal effect of the gradual oxidation of the oil by constantly using bitumen as an undertone and glaze. Melville used literary bitumen in a similar fashion.

*

* *

We have had more than enough of what Wyndham Lewis called the "cult of the savage and the child." The cult of *Huckleberry Finn* is the cult of both; yet, according to Mencken, this is our only classic, and Hemingway says, "It's the best book we have. All American writing comes from that."

I think I appreciate Huckleberry Finn, and I respond to the poetry amid which he sits enthroned like an unkempt cherub on a summer cloud. Moreover, I know how he felt, for there have been many times when, "cramped up and smothery," I too have longed for the salubrious barrel and the raft. It is easy to understand how Mencken could say that his discovery of this book was the most stupendous event of his younger days.

Huckleberry Finn is unique as a book of boys, for boys, by a boy. But, if it were our only classic, we should be obliged to feel that we have only a boy for our Faust and our Don Quixote. That may perhaps be the trouble with the American mind. In any case, it strikes me as a pity, especially as we have had a Leather-Stocking.

*
* *

Mark Twain was equally notable for badness of judgment and goodness of heart. He ridiculed the notion that the redmen had any poetry in them, and he could never deride sufficiently the "Fenimore Cooper Indians."

Of course, he had the frontiersman's prejudice against them. This prejudice destroyed his judgment, for, regarding the poetry of the Indians, Fenimore Cooper was ten times closer to the truth than Mark Twain.

But Mark Twain was too good-hearted to maintain for long a grudge against any variety of under-dog. It was a Paiute Indian he had known in California who was present to receive Captain Stormfield when he visited heaven.

*

* *

According to John Eglinton (in *Irish Literary Portraits*) the question, "Is Prescott or Motley the better writer?" was one that George Moore liked to spring on his friends in Dublin. Parkman was never included in this question, in Ireland or anywhere else in Europe, although he was perhaps a better writer than either. This was because Europeans were not interested in his subject-matter: they preferred to read about the Netherlands and Spain, and they did not care for American characters or themes. Nor was Park-

man read in his own time in America as Prescott and
Motley had been read. Where these had both been
sold in the tens of thousands, Parkman was printed
in editions of a few hundreds, for the history of Spain
and the Netherlands interested Americans in those
days far more than the history of their own country.
John Fiske bore eloquent testimony to this fact.

To a large extent, the vogue of novelists is also
determined by their subject-matter, although few readers nowadays would be willing to admit it; for the
modern reader believes he is governed by considera-
tions of form alone and critics speak of the "heresy of
the subject." Yet there may still be readers who dis-
like Dickens because he wrote about common people,
as others used to love Thackeray because he loved a
lord; and did not Henry James admit a somewhat similar preference in one of his conversations with Edith
Wharton? He said he preferred Tolstoy to *Madame
Bovary* because "one paints the fierce passions of a
luxurious aristocracy, while the other deals with the
petty miseries of a little bourgeoise in a provincial
town."

Granting that James, as a novelist, was greater than
Howells, the all but total oblivion that befell the
latter after his death can only be explained in some
such fashion. "I don't like Howells's books because I

detest the kind of people he writes about," Lafcadio Hearn remarked to a correspondent, and, while the English seldom cared to read about Americans, the Americans were apt to prefer Anthony Trollope. This was not because Trollope was infinitely better than Howells but because they were fascinated by Trollope's people.

*
* *

The old Southern romancer James Lane Allen lamented in one of his essays that we had no "gentleman" characters in American fiction, or at least that there were no Roger de Coverleys or Colonel Newcomes among our generally known fictional types. He said that "Uncle Tom" and "Uncle Remus," servants both, were the only figures in our fiction that were known throughout the world, though he should have added Natty Bumppo and, a generation later, he would have been obliged to add Huckleberry Finn. But these would not have altered the generalization.

It is certainly true that the gentleman has figured rarely in American fiction, especially fiction on the highest imaginative level, and I would say that the only conceivable reason for this is that the American "unconscious" has been otherwise engaged. On the conscious level Fenimore Cooper was aristocratic in his sympathies and tastes, and many of his characters were people of the educated classes; but who remembers any of them beside the sailors, Indians and scouts who sprang out of what we call the writer's "genius"? These were all men of the humbler sort, like Melville's "kingly commons," like the farmers, mechanics and ferrymen whom Whitman admired, like Mark Twain's pilots and river folk, like Audubon's foresters and pioneers, Bret Harte's stage-drivers and the fishermen of Winslow Homer. The American genius, to call it so, seems to possess a strong bent for admiring simple people and seeing in them what Emerson called "gods in low disguises,"—for seeing the potential, in short, in the natural germ, and I would say that if anything indicates the profound uniqueness of American life it is this obvious tendency of the American unconscious. Is this not still marked in the plays of Eugene O'Neill? How trite and flavourless is the speech of his upper-class characters, and how alive and poetic his language becomes when he falls into the argot of the slums and of common sailors.

Does this not prove the reality of the "collective unconscious," in terms of nationality, at least? And it strikes me that another aspect of our literature illustrates this,—its apparent indifference or hostility to the "big" business man. Allan Nevins recently remarked that Andrew Carnegie and Rockefeller were larger men than American writers have thought, and another commentator says that the American business man has been misrepresented in our fiction. Of course there are many good business men, as there are many gentlemen, in the America we know, but here again the oracles are dumb. The unconscious does not respond to the stimulus in question, and I am not convinced of the contrary by the crop of current novels that find much to praise in the heroes of the profit system. Not one of them has the authority of Frank Norris's *The Octopus* or of Sinclair Lewis's *Babbitt* or Dos Passos's *The Big Money*. It was still possible in 1880 for Howells to convey in *Silas Lapham* the feeling of business as the "romance, the poetry of our time,"—to convey Lapham's own feeling of the "poetry of paint,"—but only in Sinclair Lewis's *Dodsworth* and Booth Tarkington's *The Plutocrat* have novelists admiringly pictured the big business man since. Theodore Dreiser's Cowperwood presented the feeling that is general with writers about this conspicuous familiar American type, that he can survive very well without help from them, for all the big battalions are on the side of business now, just as they were in the days of Mark Hanna. When, with its advertising interests, it largely controls the radio and the press, imposing conformity of opinion, opposing free speech, how can one expect the unconscious of writers to produce lively images of the business man as hero?

VIII

NOTES ON CRITICISM

AMIEL, defining the critic, the "true critic" that none of us can ever hope to become, remarks, "What years of labour, what study and comparison, are needed to bring the critical judgment to maturity!" Only at fifty, he adds, can the critic "have made the round of all the modes of being, only by then can he have mastered all the possible shades of appreciation." Only, one might rather say, when he has lived as long as the Wandering Jew. As for the early fruit of a critic's mind, it can hardly be other than green. When, growing older, we lose our greenness, the danger is that we may not acquire the famous *lumen siccum* that parches and offends, as Bacon says, "most men's watery or soft natures," a light that is valuable not because it is dry, but because, being dry, it is closest to fire.

*
* *

Especially in a time like ours,—a time of wars and rumours of wars,—any suggestion of the easy-going is

intolerable in a writer. To be bland is to be damned
in the eyes of critics, whom geniality fills with a fury
of contempt, for they share generally Baudelaire's dis-
like of the *style coulant*,—the flowing style,—that was
beloved by his contemporaries Turgenev and Renan.
T. E. Hulme set the tone of this epoch when he said,
"Smoothness—hate it. This is the obsession that starts
all my theories." Why Hulme came to feel this way
is a question for a biographer, and it would be an
interesting question to examine, but he struck a key-
note of the coming time when he expressed this feeling at the outset of the first world war. For the flowing
style, suggesting facility, and sometimes even sales-
manship, is felt to be incompatible with a sense of the
tragic; and a time of troubles, as Lewis Mumford
says, requires, above everything, concentration. "Under
these circumstances, every word that is uttered must
be handed out sparingly, like the rounds of ammuni-
tion in a besieged fortress . . . Only words that will
enable [people] to command their energies more effec-
tively have a right to be heard at such moments."
At these times austerity becomes the mode in language,
and the *style coulant* goes out with "romantic criticism."

*

*   *

In criticism, no faint praise. Take away from the author everything that is not his by right, take it as a surgeon takes away every last cell of morbid tissue, with a strict and relentless knife; then cauterize the wound and help the victim to his feet again and send him away with both hands filled with flowers.

An author whose tissue is so morbid that he cannot survive the operation should not be subjected to it. He should be allowed to die in peace.

*
* *

In view of the mistakes he is always making, a critic should wear sackcloth as his everyday garment.

*
* *

No one is fit to judge a book until he has rounded Cape Horn in a sailing vessel, until he has bumped into two or three icebergs, until he has been lost in the sands of the desert, until he has spent a few years in the House of the Dead.

*
* *

Sainte-Beuve, in his essay on Leopardi, apologizes for writing of a foreign author, persuaded as he is that literary criticism has "its full value and originality" only when it applies itself "to subjects of which, through immediate contact and from a long way back, it possesses the source, the surrounding facts and all the circumstances." The poet Yeats had a similar thought when he wrote, "One can only reach out to the universe with a gloved hand,—that hand is one's nation, the only thing that one knows even a little about." As for Sainte-Beuve, he wrote about various foreign authors with surpassing skill and understanding, and yet it seems to me that he stated a principle here to which a critic may well give heed in his practice.

*

*   *

We all know those critics who, as Elie Faure said, "spend their time looking for fleas in the lion's mane."

*

*   *

My chief complaint against what is called scholarship in the United States,—in which we seem almost to have supplanted the Germans,—is that, like a certain person of whom Emily Dickinson wrote, it has "the facts but not the phosphorescence of learning."

*
* *

My ancient friend Francis Grierson remarked in one
of his essays, "Many writers are slow to praise, fear-
ing that frank enthusiasm will be taken as a mark of
critical incapacity." Yet few demur at wholesale con-
demnation. For most readers destructive critics are
naturally impressive and they somehow feel it is more
perspicacious to detect imperfections and weaknesses
than it is to point out merits. Actually, "star-finding,"
as Frank Harris called it, requires a far greater acumen
and skill. This is a point to remember at a time when
appreciation is virtually a forgotten word in critical
circles.

*
* *

There are critical circles in which ignorance and low
vitality pass for superior discrimination, circles in which
one stands high if one has read only the writers in
fashion,—provided one does not like even these too
much.

*
* *

What criticism lacks nowadays is precisely the heart
of the matter. William Morris did not say all, but how

much he said, as he rubbed with both hands the part
of his waistcoat that covered the seat of his diaphragm,
"I always know when a thing is really good by its
making me feel warm across here."

*

* *

Have there ever been such literary spoil-sports as the
formalist critics? I used to think that half the pleasure
of being a Californian would be that one had come
from Bret Harte's country; for, with all his occasional
crudity, Bret Harte invested with magic the Sierras,
the bay of San Francisco and the Sacramento River.
But could any such feeling survive, in the mind of
a young Californian, the discipline of these academic
fashionable critics? They would condition him to see
only the ways in which Bret Harte fell short of the
formal virtues of the models they study, and all the
magic he might have found in his story-telling coun-
tryman would have died in a clatter of analysis and
scientific prosing. How many literary windows these
critics have closed! How much they have destroyed of
the savour and flavour that literature has always im-
parted to society and life! Wherever we live we should
cherish especially the writers who have added another

dimension to the country that has chosen us or that
we have chosen.

*
*   *

The Germans have destroyed their language "because
they work in silence and because the life of literature
is conversation." So John Jay Chapman once remarked,
and is this not the trouble with the formalist critics,
the new grammarians, who write in their esoteric magazines? I mean those whom Kenneth Burke calls the
"critics-who-write-critiques-of-critical-criticism." Thanks
to them, the larger the popular view of the world becomes,—planetary or global, as one chooses to call it,—
the smaller becomes the horizon of the critical mind.
For they make literary mincemeat of the greatest matters. They too work in silence, for one cannot imagine them reading aloud their wire-drawn cerebrations,
nor can one imagine a woman listening to them. They
are also too much the victims of the air they breathe.
"University air, court air and such other bad and
vitiated atmospheres that separate one from the free
and sunny daylight of ordinary people must either be
avoided altogether or at least breathed for short periods only." So said one of the writers of "Young

Germany" in the days of Heine, and he might have
been speaking with the formalist critics in mind.

*

* *

One of the reviewers in a New York weekly pointed
out recently that a certain literary "revival" was all a
mistake, for the book that was the basis of it, a monu-
mental *succès d'estime*, was by no means a great
original work of genius. The reviewer suggested that
the author, far from being an innovator, was an imitator in theme, technique and character alike and that
he had modelled his whole work, in every essential
respect, on Anatole France's "Monsieur Bergeret"
series.

Assuming that the reviewer is not mistaken, what
a light this throws on our present world of critics!—
a world in which it goes without saying that Anatole
France is forgotten, like virtually all but a handful of
writers in vogue. From the moment when Paul Valéry
scouted him on a famous occasion, Anatole France
passed more and more out of notice, and his justice-
loving Voltairean spirit was in any case anathema to
the mediævalizing mind of the years that followed.
And Anatole France is only one of a host of great
writers who have been pushed aside as the critics,

examining texts, have lost themselves in Henry James's cloudy crystal ball, while, between pedantry on one hand and on the other primitivism, general literary knowledge has all but disappeared. We have seen old-fashioned Confederate novels hailed as original that were merely Mary Johnston served up cold, because no one remembers Mary Johnston, and a novel that was second-rate Booth Tarkington was recently called "revolutionary" because no one knows Booth Tarkington in highbrow circles. The formalist critics have made passive war on general literary knowledge, and without this knowledge how can we form judgments at all?

*

* *

Some day critics of poetry will once more quote with approval Anatole France's phrase in *The Garden of Epicurus*: "Poets must not be too keen to argue about the laws of their art; when they lose their innocence their charm goes with it, and like fish out of water they flounder helplessly in the arid regions of theory."

*

* *

Let me quote three statements by three scholarly authors and leave them, in this order, to speak for themselves:

"The historians Motley, Prescott, Bancroft, Parkman, Rhodes, Lea, Fiske were not professors: books like Taylor's *The Mediæval Mind*, Henry Adams's *Mont St. Michel and Chartres*, Thayer's *Cavour*, Villard's *John Brown* and Beveridge's *John Marshall*, even Ticknor's history of Spanish literature were not written within college walls."—J. E. Spingarn, *Creative Criticism and Other Essays*.

"Such as they are [my own books], I could not have written them had my time been taken by teaching or academic administration."—Henry Osborn Taylor, *A Layman's View of History*.

"I soon learned [as an editor] that it was virtually impossible to get fair consideration for a book written by a scholar not connected with a university from a reviewer so connected. Invariably the review, if it did not damn outright and outrageously, would begin by saying that for an amateur the work was commendable, but . . . Envy seems to have abundant place in the present halls of Academe."—Paul Elmer More, *With the Wits*.

*

* *

One should be wary of terms that end in *ism*,—Classicism, Romanticism, Naturalism and the like. Many of these terms should go back to the button-moulder, for they are played out. A critic in our time should either mint new phrases or explain in what sense he uses the old ones.

These classifications are not for imaginative minds, though they form the stock-in-trade of so many critics, and in certain cases they are of recent origin, and not invariably a creditable origin at that. Consider Zola's comment on "Naturalism," as reported in the Goncourt Journal: "Let me tell you that I care no more about the word Naturalism than you do; nevertheless, I shall continue to use it, because it is necessary to baptise things in order that the public may think them new."

One should reconceive the states of mind and the tones of feeling that lie behind these labels. Every real writer partakes of the nature of all these categories and is partly romantic, partly naturalistic, classical, humanistic and all the rest.

*
* *

I cannot accept the oft-quoted remark of a contemporary critic that "literature is neither religion nor social engineering." *The Imitation of Christ* is both religion and literature, and are not Plato's *Republic* and Sir Thomas More's *Utopia* both literature and social engineering? Literature may be anything and everything; and what remains when they tell us what it is *not*? They reduce it to the proverbial more and more about nothing.

*

*   *

Because he is dictatorial Eliot appeals all the more to an age that desires orthodoxy and desires to conform. How could such an age not wish for a literary pope?

*

*   *

I note that Robert Frost is now called a "popular" poet by critics for whom this word is the last word of contempt. It is a fixed idea with them that, as Edwin Muir says, "The imaginative writer today can be widely popular only by writing falsely," and the fact that a writer appeals to a large number of readers is in itself sufficient to condemn him. I have seen this idea repeated by at least one member of the avant-garde who has in the meantime become a best-seller, as Henry Adams became a best-seller when his *Education* was finally published and George Santayana when he wrote a novel. Have we not seen Eliot a popular playwright and writer for the screen with an audience almost as large as Hemingway's?—"the largest immediate audience ever reached by a serious writer," as *Time* said when he published *The Old Man and the Sea.*

This mode of criticism by numbers is a curious development of the literary fashion-making mind, all the stranger at a time when William Faulkner's novels repeatedly appear in a series called "good reading for the millions." The idea persists in it that a writer must be inferior if he has more than about five thousand readers, and that everything has changed in this respect since the days of Mark Twain or of Thackeray and Dickens. But, with Faulkner selling like bags of peanuts and in view of the enormous sales of Scott Fitzgerald, Wolfe and so many others, how can we feel that the question of numbers means more or less in our time than it meant fifty or a hundred years ago? As often as not, the best books have been the most popular books, and is that not really all one can say on the subject? How vast was the contemporary popularity of *The Red Badge of Courage* and of Frank Norris's *The Octopus* a few years later. Norris's book was so popular, in fact, that, in order to live undisturbed in Chicago, when he was preparing to write *The Pit,* he was obliged to go into hiding in the town.

I suggest that this notion is a delayed reaction from

the nineteenth-century worship of numbers that Matthew Arnold deplored in one of his essays. It springs from an anti-commercial instinct that is deep in the minds of American writers and quite distorts their feeling for the reality of the matter. The fact is that popularity or the reverse of popularity has no connection whatever with the merit of a book. Generally speaking, popular books have two traits in common, a subject of central human interest and a certain vitality in the presentation, and these traits may be found equally in good books and bad. Meanwhile, to call Frost a popular poet, using the word in a derogatory sense, is to keep in reserve no word for common rhymesters.

*

*   *

"Pissarro's letters remind me that no artist should paint to sell." So says John Sloan, the painter, in one of his notes. "I am always a little shocked to find that these independent French artists expected to make a living from their pictures. Even Millet,—so poor and with a large family to support,—never considered any other way of making a living."

This indicates an American trait, one we have developed because we live in a society in which money "talks." Because it talks and talks so much, American artists shrink from it, and even the mere idea of it, like no others in the world, and I suppose that John Sloan would have thought less of himself if he had made a living, or a good living, from his pictures. If, like Picasso, he had made a million dollars, he would have lost all faith in his integrity and talent. This is the psychological twist that has driven into communism so many Americans who have made money in the arts.

I call this an American trait,—along with the superstition regarding popularity and numbers,—because our writers share it, and an English friend, a novelist who is interested in the "cash nexus" of writing, tells me that American writers are "incurably genteel." He writes to me, "They pretend there is no cash nexus," adding, "It is bad manners in the United States even to allude to what a man gets for his work." It is true that in all this we are rather prudish, but it is because in this country the commercial world intrudes into every sphere of life. The English mind is safer, or perhaps one should say it used to be, and is therefore freer. Samuel Butler had the same unaffected interest in money that Dr. Johnson had and that my friend has; and Trollope, who felt "somewhat as I suppose . . . an undertaker feels when he is called upon

to supply a funeral," did not hesitate to "make money-
return a first object." Then there was Virginia Woolf,
who was almost obsessed with the question of the
sales of her books. Not one of these writers was ever
corrupted either by having this interest or professing
it frankly.

Still, I like our rather airy American notions. They
keep alive the feeling that poverty and good work are
somehow allied, a valuable feeling where money talks
too much.

*
* *

The most serious charge that critics can bring against
a writer nowadays is to say that he is naive, and yet
something like naivety is rapidly becoming the one
thing necessary for writers. Or perhaps the right word
is ingenuousness, for I do not recommend the un-
tutored, the too artless or the provincial. What I do
mean is the opposite of the kind of sophistical knowingness that chokes so much of the writing of this
generation. The literary mind of our day reflects the
general urban mind in being, in all respects, over-
conscious, while the mass-influences of advertising,
analysis, cosmetics and Kinsey reports have worn away
its freshness and destroyed its bloom. In consequence

it has lost the capacity for wonder that is so essential to the poet and the story-teller. What was it that accounted for Dylan Thomas's unique position among the younger poets of the time? Precisely that he had escaped the sophistication that has paralyzed the contemporary poetic mind. He seemed to be uniquely capable of both wonder and joy. The capacity for wonder presupposes a certain childlikeness that has lost its value today in both literature and life.

One of my correspondents wrote to me the other day that "the young writers of America are old and dangerous." From that frame of mind how can writing emerge? When no one speaks of the heart any longer except as a physical organ, and few seem to know the difference between love and sex, what becomes inevitably of natural feeling? And without natural feeling there can be no wonder, the kind of wonder that gave Theodore Dreiser, banal and material as he was, the sense that, in life and the world, he was "a guest at a feast." He found wonderlands on all sides, in newspaper offices, in factory buildings, in shop-girls brushing their hair at open windows, and for his readers too this wonder invested with magic the spectacle of everyday existence. It was this kind of ingenuousness that redeemed Dreiser,—the gift of being surprised by things, of looking at the world "with eyes wide open in wonder," as Ortega put it.

The painter's innocence of the eye belongs in this way to the writer too, and how right Amiel was in saying, "The novelist must be ingenuous, at least when his pen is in his hand." For this innocence is the spring of all clear perception, and the question is "how to regain the naive or innocent soul," as D. H. Lawrence said in one of his letters. "How to make it," he continued, "the man within the man,—your 'societal'; and at the same time keep the cognitive mode for defences and adjustments and 'work'." No one can tell how far writers are capable of this again until the gospel of knowingness has worn itself out, in criticism, in the general atmosphere that writers breathe. The ideal of the knowing man, which tends to dominate the modern writer, is altogether foreign to his true nature.

Mencius said that a wise man should somehow keep the childlike mind. What a rebuke that is to our tiresome American ideal of "sophistication."

IX

MOSTLY PERSONAL

WHAT curious tricks our minds play on us. Looking up from my work, I saw a fly crawling on the window-pane. Then I saw that he was crawling between the window-pane and the storm-window outside it, and I knew he could never escape from this huge glass trap. At once I began to sympathize with him, toiling over this desert of glass with nothing to eat or drink day after day, and at last I walked over to the inner window and raised it so that this fellow-creature might be delivered from so sad a fate. "To open the window and let a wasp out,—ah, is this not happiness?" a Chinese writer once exclaimed; and who forgets Uncle Toby in *Tristram Shandy*?—when, catching the fly that tormented him, he thrust it out of the window, saying, "Get thee gone, poor devil! Why should I harm thee? The world is surely large enough for thee and me."

But how short-lived in me was this noble feeling. No sooner had I opened the inner window than it struck me that this fellow-creature had become simply a fly in my study, and I knew he would soon be buzzing about my ears. All my tender feelings suddenly turned cold,—I forgot Uncle Toby and the Chinese poet,—and before I knew what I was doing I had crushed that fly.

*
* *

I use about a quart of ink a year. I like black ink, as Kipling did,—"the blackest." All blue-blacks are an abomination to my dæmon.

It appears, however, that most Americans like blue ink, which, as an advertisement says, is so much better "because it turns black in six months." Evidently, the leisurely business men who patronize this ink like to wait six months for their effects, but with me, as a writer, time presses. When I make tracks on paper, I wish to see them, and black ink is very hard to find. Every time I try to get it I go through the same procedure and end by accepting a compromise that leaves me in doubt, for black has turned to "coal black," or "coal" black to "koal" black,—the last form it assumed was "midnight" black. All these words protest too much, arousing in me a painful scepticism. Is "coal" black as black as black?—is it blacker or less black if the "coal" is "koal"?—and is not "midnight" black really purple? As in everything else in our country, we cannot let well enough alone but must have something new at any price. (I now see a fluid advertised as "successor to ink.") The baser explanation of this is that the manufacturers are always trying to get ahead of their rivals, who might spring something new on the world if they did not spring it first; but the manufacturers favour a nobler explanation,—that all this represents a thirst for perfection. From their point of view, "midnight" black stands for one of the phases of a toilsome process. The next phase may well be the black of "just before dawn," while mere black will remain as a primitive taste of a prehistoric race that knew no better. It is the law of life in a business world that nothing shall continue in one stay; but, while the improvers affirm that the bad gets better, it appears to me that the good gets worse. *Verweile doch! du bist so schön!* goes for ink as for everything else in a world in which business motives are too good to be true.

*
* *

"Democracy in economics, aristocracy in thought." I like this phrase of A.E. My political creed is based on the assumption that everybody ought to be given a chance. My literary creed is based on the assumption that few will ever take the chance.

*
* *

Why do I wish to avoid such men as S, who abound among artists and writers? They are the men with a foot on each side of the fence, the side of their own talent and the side of the mundane. They have a superstitious regard for those who are altogether on the side of their talent, but, if they had to make a choice and plant both feet on one side of the line, they would undoubtedly take the side of the mundane. This tormented double-mindedness subtly poisons the air about them. I know how to deal with the frankly worldly, but these half-artists, soft within, affect me like stretches of marsh-land. You never know, in their presence, where to place your feet and you begin to doubt your own ground. They *give* at every point, and, meeting no resistance, your muscles begin to seem illusory. It does not do to linger after nightfall in swamps of this kind. One is in danger of catching malaria in them.

*
* *

I am naturally drawn to painters. They are just like writers, without the nonsense. Of course, they have their own nonsense, but I don't have to bother about that.

Why do artists of every kind gravitate to painters? Perhaps because they are apt to be simple and happy. As Virgil Thomson says, in *The State of Music*, "The Seeing Eye has no opinions" and "The painter's whole morality consists in keeping his brushes clean and getting up in the morning." Therefore, painters are "a pleasant lot, cheerful and healthy." So it is inevitable that the rest of us, writers, musicians and what not, who are so often morbid, are drawn to painters.

*

* *

The first time I met Sam Lewisohn, the great art-collector, he said to me, "What do you consider the greatest American picture?"—"Why," said I, "Albert Ryder's 'Jonah and the Whale.'"—"How did you guess it?" said he. The second time I met him, he asked the same question and I gave the same reply. The third time he did not ask the question but simply began to talk about Albert Ryder.

My reply was almost automatic, for I had never thought of the matter before; but, having once thought and said it, I continued to think that Ryder's 'Jonah' is the greatest American picture. In fact, having merely thought it, I became sure of it because a well-qualified person was of my opinion. How many of our certitudes are bred in that way in the mind.

*

*   *

I received this morning a warranty deed entitling me to a piece of land that I have long desired and am glad to own. Yet, strangely, when I saw my name inscribed upon this deed, I felt a tremor in my bones. This deed was full of a kind of poetry. I became a grantee, with "assigns forever." The land was mine, for my "own proper use and behoof." With the "ensealing of these presents," I was "well seized of the premises." My estate was indefeasible "in fee simple." I was henceforth entitled to privileges, appurtenances and all manner of other high and mighty rights in regard to bargaining and selling, and the grantor was bound to defend me. I had a feeling of pride in associating my name with these admirable phrases, this poetry of the law that carries me back directly to the lives of my Saxon forbears in their mud-huts and manors,— for, like everyone of my name, I had forbears in both. Well I know what all these phrases have represented in terms of toil and sweat and self-respect for untold generations of these forbears, what struggles and triumphs they have stood for and what a large portion of history in this country and England. And yet I felt a tremor in my bones.

For my instinct does not claim property, however I may rejoice in it. I have another kind of estate to which it is inimical. All men are tamed nomads, born to wander after adventure, and this is especially true in the case of writers. They are, and must be, sojourners on the earth, and they dread the trap of property, the trap of possessions. Writers in their hearts are like Arabs and soldiers, and Tolstoy stood for them all when he ran away at the end of his life, preferring to die in a railway station or on the open road. How well I understand my friend the sailor-novelist, who cannot bear to see a garden planted round his house. For him every shoot is a nail that holds him in place. His rolling fields remind him of the waves, and he longs to be off again.

*

* *

On my afternoon walks in winter, I always receive the same impression from the effect of the sunlight on the farmhouse window-panes. It is the winter light of four or five o'clock, and it produces in me an indefinable sense of desolation, like the whistle of the railway trains in wide empty spaces of sea-coast or prairie. I am stricken at once with a lonely feeling, as if I were abandoned in the void between the worlds. Byron must have had this feeling when he wrote some of the passages in *Cain* and *Manfred*.

Charles Burchfield catches this effect of light on the window-panes of the forsaken houses that he paints in so many of his water-colours, and I find a word that conveys my sensation in one of the old Vermont ballads:

> Till when at length he reached the cabin,
>   Black and desolate it stood;
> Cold the hearth and windows *ralist*
>   In their stillest solitude.

This is the "certain slant of light on winter afternoons" that Emily Dickinson describes in one of her poems. She says it is "like the distance on the look of death."

*

* *

R.B. has been telling me of an Indian footpath he used to see as a boy, along the Delaware river, near Trenton. It was clearly marked, although hidden by the underbrush, and the local woodsman who showed him where to find it had traced this path miles north-ward until it joined the old Mohawk trail.

Nothing catches more at one's imagination than these ancient paths, which are apparently never oblit-erated,—like the path round Walden pond in Concord, "worn by the feet of Indian hunters," as Thoreau says. In Concord there is another path, along the ridge by the Boston road, which Hawthorne wore with his feet, during his last brooding years, and which was still clearly marked ninety years later. Prescott wore a similar path at Lynn, where he had a summer villa. There was a cherry-tree beside the house, and he plodded round and round this tree for hours every day. He could not, in his blindness, venture further, and the shade of the cherry-tree protected his eyes. The traces of this path remained for many years.

I knew well a path like this in the garden of a California house where I spent several years, a path that had not been used for a century or more. It was worn by the Franciscan monks of the mission and was said to have led to a spring. In England, at various times, I have seen traces of two long disused Roman roads, one from Shooter's Hill, the other from one of the Sussex downs. They were invisible on the plain, even if one happened to walk along them, but easily seen from above, although they were both covered with waving grain. Or am I mistaken in thinking that the Sussex road was a Roman road? It may have been the one that Kipling speaks of,—

> See you the dimpled track that runs
> All hollow through the wheat?
> O that was where they hauled the guns
> That smote King Philip's fleet.

However it may have been, Elizabethan or Roman, the plough, during all these hundreds of years, had stirred only the earth on the surface. The subsoil had remained so packed by the traffic of those far-off days that the grain in the ruts still grew in a different fashion from the surrounding grain. Mary Austin told me it was the same way with the pioneer trails over the Western deserts, that a road, once thoroughly beaten, however long disused, was never quite blotted out.

*
* *

How much a simple phrase, rightly remembered, can mean. My old friend in England, S.E., went to school with a son of Matthew Arnold and visited the Arnolds on one of his vacations. He remembered how the great man entered a room, and, lifting his left hand, waved it in the direction of the awe-struck boys, saying, in a sweetly deprecating sing-song voice, "You may sit down." As much of Arnold lingers for me in this picture as there was of conduct in his theory of life, not that I disagree with the theory of conduct.

There also comes back to me a phrase uttered by Charles Eliot Norton on one of his "Dante evenings" at Shady Hill, perhaps when the sherry was being passed, with the little silver basket of caraway cakes. It was to the effect that the picture of heaven in the Book of Revelation,—with its excess of precious stones,—was such as might have been conceived "by a New York woman." What a phrase was that for expressing how Boston and Cambridge felt about the gaudy New York splendours that had vulgarized their beloved old Newport.

Still a third phrase comes back, in a reminiscence of my childhood. It evokes my great-grandfather's house, —of which I used to hear much,—where Horace Greeley was lunching on one of his political journeys. "You can be fixing me some" was the phrase, in reply to a question of his hostess, whether he would have a little salad,—uttered no doubt with one of his hands in the butter and his honest pumpkin face shining over all.

*

*   *

When I was in college, Theodore Roosevelt came to tea at the *Advocate,* of which he too had been an editor once. This was my first experience of animal magnetism raised to the proportions of the jungle, for one could feel his presence approaching down the corridor, before he came in sight, "like echoes whispering where great armies be." Another guest was there, the English author W. H. Mallock, who had written *The New Republic.* Roosevelt, hearing his name, grasped his hand; and then, although the meeting was quite impromptu, he poured forth a flood of comment on Mallock's views and books, every one of which he seemed to have read and remembered. It was like Niagara falling on a fern, for the little old man was stunned with confusion and pleasure. Since then, I have never had a doubt that Theodore Roosevelt, whatever else he was, was a portent and really a man of genius.

*

* *

Twice I saw Swinburne in the flesh, performing an act, moreover, that he celebrated in a score of rondels of his own composition,—not to mention various odes, ballades and sonnets. What was the act? Playing with

the toes of a baby. Every day, at eleven in the morning, Swinburne clicked the gate of The Pines behind
him and marched up Putney Hill and across Wimble-
don Common and sat him down at a public-house with
a bottle of Shakespeare's "brown October." And it was
on Putney Hill that the act occurred, two, three or
four minutes after eleven.

Was it an unworthy instinct that led me to play the
spy and saunter along the pavement across the street,
pretending I did not know that I was within twenty
yards of the greatest poet living in the world? (For I
so thought him then.) I heard the door of The Pines
open and shut; with the tail of my eye I saw the little
figure coming down the path. He swung the gate,
made a sharp turn to the left and then began his progress up the hill.

What an odd little apparition,—like a toy soldier,
tiny and shiny, exactly as if he had just come out of
a box. The prodigious head, with the reddish nose and
the white and yellow beard, was crowned by a turban,
a big white turban with a brim, and the neat little
military figure, stiff and straight, with the great cir-
cular watch-chain, rose out of varnished boots that
twinkled as he walked. In his gait he suggested a
mechanical puppet, and his arms swung with the pre-

cision of a miniature grenadier on parade. One seemed to see Watts-Dunton, in the shadows behind him, winding him up for the day.

Then one foresaw that the act was about to happen. Down the hill moved a perambulator, propelled by a nurse in a long blue cape and a cap with streamers. It was evident that she was prepared for the ceremony. She stopped, she waited, and presently the poet was abreast of her. Suddenly he turned to the right and bent from the middle. Up came the forearm, down went the hand, then the prodigious head plunged, and nose, beard, turban, brim and all were lost among the pillows. To the chanting of the birds, in the eye of the morning sun, Algernon Charles Swinburne, naughty poet of secrecy and shade, perverse lover of how many an evil-flowering feminine ghost, had caught and kissed the toes of the baby. And who could doubt that, marching on, he plotted another rondel on that same theme, to be written down as he sat in the public-house over the bottle of "glorious British beer"?

X

AFTERTHOUGHTS

ONE is a long time finding out how different others are from oneself, and what wildly improbable lives, from one's own point of view, can still be happy lives. I, who could be happy in a tub, or on St. Simeon's pillar, if certain things were right with me, think other people are queer; and I am always relieved to learn that they like their queerness.

*
* *

I used to be impressed by people who gave themselves out as persons of large importance. In this regard, the serpent of doubt entered my garden only when I reached years of discretion. Judging by the mask and gown, the beetling brow, the gesture of command, I imagined in earlier days that I had encountered all manner of great men along my path.

In later years I found that genius and virtue more often clothe themselves in hodden grey than in the splendid feathers of macaws and peacocks. Corneille looked like a cattle-dealer, and Descartes might have been taken for an honest Dutch merchant,—or so says Balzac in *Illusions perdues,*—while visitors to La Brède, meeting Montesquieu in a cotton nightcap, carrying a rake on his shoulder, mistook him for a gardener. They followed in this the law of protective coloration, which is based upon another law, that of the conservation of energy. It takes a great deal of energy to maintain an appearance of greatness, more than the really great are able to spare.

*

* *

A Well-Connected Man. I once knew a man, well-connected in New York, who bore the name of a great Spanish painter. I asked him if he was related to the Spanish painter. "Oh yes," he said, "he was a distant cousin but he belonged to the peasant branch of the family."

*

* *

What a strange separation of faculties is possible in a human being. L., as a man, is the soul of both honour and kindness, yet intellectually,—and I speak by the book,—he is at the same time a fool and a knave.

*

* *

An evening with three eminent men of law. They began to speak of literature, in all amiability, and then what a pulling out of chestnuts, fossilized for ages in the legal mind, half the familiar quotations from Bartlett, chiefly from Pope, and the question rose, "Who wrote Junius?" It was evident that one and all were talking as they thought lawyers ought to talk, that they were following the well-known pattern of the learned judge unbending. What children are these great men, so exactly living up to the parts that conventional public opinion expects them to play.

In *Fors Clavigera*, Ruskin relents towards lawyers enough to admit them to a "dignified almshouse," because they are picturesque,—"for the sake of their wigs." I should preserve them for another reason, but also one that springs from a love of the past. For as long as lawyers exist, Bartlett's "familiar quotations" will never be unfamiliar.

*

* *

I like R.R.'s story about his Boston friend who, when he comes to New York and settles in the great metropolitan hotel, opens his parcels and puts away in a drawer every scrap of wrapping-paper and every fragment of string,—so they will not be "lonely" until he can take them back to Boston.

*
* *

"The younger generation." All generations are alike when they are younger, and all the older generations have said the same things about them. What could one add to the comment of Pliny the Younger, when he had become the older?—it fairly describes my generation when I was twenty-one: "Which of them pays submission as an inferior to age or authority? These young gentlemen begin life as sages; they know everything from the outset; and there is no one they revere or imitate, for they are themselves the only models which they are disposed to follow." (*Letters,* VIII, 23.)

*
* *

Why is it that English literary genius seems to develop better than ours, or has appeared in the past to develop better? Perhaps because in England literary genius develops within known metes and bounds. It is obliged in most ways to conform instead of following its nose in all directions, as it does in our more fluid and open country. This is not, but it might have been what Goethe meant when he spoke of the limits within which the master declares himself.

*
* *

How confidently English writers count on fame! Cun-
ninghame Graham, for instance, writing of W. H.
Hudson, spoke of his place in literature as "fixed as
securely as Betelgeuse in the firmament." He called
Far Away and Long Ago "a classic as imperishable"
as the stories that Boccaccio penned for mankind's delight, and he could use these words in a country in
which literary men arrive at an "assured status" with
the age of eighty. For so I read in a trustworthy English review, which also informs me that three books
on Norman Douglas have been published within a
year of this author's death. In England what centenary
of an author goes unnoticed? There statues of authors
are erected in towns where they have lived, there
tablets are affixed to their houses, there plays are written and acted about them and memorial editions, ten
volumes at a time, are published in "Penguins" ten
years after their death.

In this country the hungry generations tread them
down, and no writer of any kind is able to count on
a public that will remain loyal for ten or even for
three years. In literature we have few permanent titles,
—there is no such thing as winning one's spurs. This

is partly because the American mind, unlike the English, is not formed by books but, as Carl Sandburg once said to me, waving a good-bye from the platform of a train, "by newspapers and the Bible." But is this something that critics can take lying down? Is it not in the interest of all of them, and of authors acting with them, to create in this country a memory and a fund of esteem?

*
* *

I remember forty years ago waking up in an English village and hearing children outside my window counting, "Eena, meana, mina, mo." These were the words that my friends and I had used in my childhood in a New Jersey town, and they were words we had never received from our elders. They belonged to a language of childhood that children had perpetuated, passing it on from one to another for I wonder how many generations, certainly ever since the days when grown-up ancient Saxons used these words instead of one, two, three. Like the pagan rites that survive in the pre-urban countryside in old Christian countries, in Italy and Spain,—of which the cultivated classes are often unaware—this prehistoric language has been preserved sub rosa, inaudible and invisible to grown-ups, by children alone.

*
* *

When, many years later, I was in England, at a sanitarium, and we cut down trees,—or cut them up,— I always by preference used an axe when all the Englishmen used saws. The doctor, observing this, remarked that his American patients had always used axes, even when the saw was more effective, and he asked me why it was. It is at least a century,—as I am surprised to find, thinking it over,—since any of my forefathers has really lived in the country; and it is nearly two centuries since any of them used an axe to build a homestead or for any essential purpose. And yet is this not plainly a case of inherited aptitude? Every American of the old stock has a pioneer backwoodsman somewhere near the beginning of his family annals, and I was amused by a passage in Tocqueville's diary of travel: "The country-dwelling Americans spend half their lives cutting trees, and their children learn at an early age to use the axe against the trees, their enemies." We Americans are axemen by instinct. We all have a Leather-Stocking under our skins.

*
*   *

We never outgrow our early chagrins. My friend
S.T. was talking once with H. G. Wells at a time
when he was already growing old. But he had never
got over the shame of being deficient in aspirates, the
stigma of the English lower classes. When he used the
word 'ope, S.T., not understanding him, innocently
asked him to repeat the word. He turned red with mor-
tification when he had to explain that he meant hope,
although he had long been a world-famous person.

My only grievance against England is that, as George
Orwell said, it is "the most caste-ridden country" in
the world, and this is a general feeling with Americans, who have no personal reason for it, inasmuch
as in England they have a status of their own. ("That's
the advantage of being an American here; you don't
belong to any class," said old Mr. Touchett, in England, in *The Portrait of a Lady*.) They are generally
quite objective when they are shocked by the English
caste-system, the "hideous class-distinctions" that, to
the elder Henry James, made "the manners of Choc-
taws," by comparison, seem "sweet and Christian."
How odd in the future will seem a system that could
so brand a man like Wells as to put him out of coun-
tenance at the height of his fame or make it appear

that the most important fact in Arnold Bennett's life was that he had a "lower middle class mind." For this is so constantly harped upon in a recent biography of Bennett that an uninformed reader might wonder if he had anything else.

Why was England, for D. H. Lawrence, so "tight and unsatisfactory" that he felt he would "die outright" if he had to live there? Was it not partly because he knew he looked like a "plumber's assistant,"—as David Garnett says in *The Golden Echo*,—and had to pay for this too large a price there?

*
* *

Historical writing in this country has virtually dropped out of literature. This is because the historians respect science more than they respect art and greatly prefer to be, or appear, scientific. But they also feel nowadays that they must know everything, psychology, economics, semantics and so on. As a result, the historical mind has been swamped with new material which it is unable to digest.

What Wordsworth said of poetry in the preface to *Lyrical Ballads* applies, in this connection, to history as well: "The remotest discoveries of the chemist, the botanist, the mineralogist, will be as proper objects of the poet's art as any upon which he is now employed, if the time should ever come when these things shall be familiar to us, and the relations under which they are contemplated shall be manifestly and palpably material to us as enjoying and suffering beings." Wordsworth meant that all subjects can serve the poet if he can apprehend them with a certain emotion, if they have become involved with his own intimate being; but that until this has occurred they cannot be turned into poetry, they cannot be transmuted into art.

Is not this the case with history also? Only when all these sciences have come to be intimately synthesized and felt will they be transmutable in this realm either. In the meantime, there is truth in Lytton Strachey's statement that "ignorance is the first requisite of a historian," the ignorance that simplifies and classifies, selects and omits. Prescott knew nothing about ethnology, Gibbon knew nothing of economics, but both have almost as many readers now as they had in the days of their first fame. When, on the other hand, one knows too much, one cannot write history, properly so called, at all.

*
* *

The method of psychoanalysis in the writing of biography has, I think, a limited value, and I believe that, having once passed, it will not be used again. If one could accept for biography Georg Brandes's dictum that, while the romantic intellect is interested in the significance of things, the modern intellect is interested only in their causes, then one might say that the day of the Plutarchs has passed and that Freud is the master of the future. But, in fact, what concerns the biographer, whether "romantic" or not, is always the significance of things. Psychoanalysis serves the psychologist in the biographer by placing him in possession of certain facts which he cannot obtain so easily by other methods. But all a biographer's facts are useless until he has reconceived them in the light of his intuitive feeling for reality and proportion. This intuitive faculty is a different mental organ from the intelligence, which actually paralyzes its operation. It is not the causes that matter in biography, it is the character itself, which belongs to the moral and aesthetic sphere, a sphere that is quite apart from the sphere of causation. The attempt to turn biography into a science is as futile as it is with history.

*

* *

The spread of science has made us feel that we ought

to be "broad-minded" and try to understand every point of view, however it may repel our natural tastes. But that does not mean that we have to accept them all. It is still more important for us to maintain the right of our natural tastes, at whatever cost in "narrow-mindedness." There are areas of thought, feeling and writing in which the proper response is Dr. Johnson's when he kicked the first object that came in his way. Kicking is an eloquent argument that may have a world of thought behind it. Every man of good sense knows when not to argue and has his mind made up on a thousand subjects that are not discussible for him. In fact, without a closed mind one cannot have an open mind. One becomes a house that has no walls, and I should not call that an open house.

*

* *

How odd it is that many people connect the classics with privilege, that they have come to think of the classics as "snobbish." One recent writer pretends, for instance, that because the word "classic" was used by the Romans to mean "classy,"—appertaining to the work of men who were property-owners,—it has not come to mean in two thousand years something wholly different, which alone counts for us. The only book I inherited from one of my grandfathers was a well-conned copy of Plutarch, which he had read as a boy on a farm; and this was rather the rule than the exception in our simple old American life of the country. Our modern wooden wagon-wheel was invented by a New Jersey farmer, who had found an exact description of it in Homer. Thomas Jefferson recorded this fact when the invention was claimed for an Englishman, and he proved that it was true. He added that the American farmers were "the only farmers who can read Homer," inasmuch as most European farmers were uneducated peasants.

So the classics will never seem "classy" to me; and democracy in fact was conceived in an aura of the classics, as much in America as in France. The American revolutionaries and the French revolutionaries met on the common ground of the Greeks and the Romans; and even long years later in France, at the time of the Restoration, it was the liberals and radicals who stood by the classics (just as our abolitionists stood by them). The royalists were all for liberty in literature, while those who stood for liberty in life upheld the strictest forms in literature. They maintained the classical forms and the classical themes, for the classical themes defended liberty, and the classical forms were the most effective. Was this not what Lucien de Rubempré found when he arrived in Paris?

Sentimental democrats may disregard the classics, but those for whom democracy is based on certain principles will find them where Thomas Paine found them.

XI

REFLECTIONS ON THE AVANT-GARDE

WHAT a fine subject for a study would be the avant-garde, which has played so large a role in modern criticism. When we ourselves are attacked by it we take pleasure in thinking unkindly of it and collecting all the unkind opinions of others. Leo Stein certainly described at least a portion of it in something that he said in *Appreciation:* "There are many people, really uncreative, who can get the illusion of creation if they are a few feet ahead of the masses, no matter how far they are behind the leaders." Leo Stein also said, more or less in this connection, "If you are doing the latest thing you can feel at least a little bit important."

Yet the avant-garde performs a valuable function. Its role is to find new talent, and to exist it must continue to find new talent periodically, at least one new talent every season. It would cease to exist after three barren seasons. To clear the decks for new talent it is obliged to assume that most established talent is obstructive and must therefore be opposed or ignored. (And ignoring talent is a way of opposing it also.) The avant-garde, moreover, can only establish new talents by giving them all the benefit of the doubt, the exact reverse of its attitude towards established talent. The word goes round that the new swan has to be a swan, even if nine swans out of ten turn out to be geese. But without the aid of the avant-garde the tenth swan might not survive at all; it might be destroyed as a chick in the prevailing inclement weather. Besides, the avant-garde is useful in perpetually changing the air that writers breathe.

*

* *

But does the avant-garde still exist? Or am I speaking of something that only "enjoys a kind of prestige among yesterday's élite"? (To quote Stravinsky's remark about Revolution.) I am told that the term first came into use, in the literary sphere, when the French took it over from the military sphere at the time of the Dreyfus case in the eighteen-nineties; and it may turn out to be a short-lived conception. In order for an avant-garde to exist, there must first exist a continuing gap between advanced and popular appreciation, together with writers of genius among the young who remain for a fairly long time unknown to the public. The heroes of the older avant-garde, among them

Eliot and Hemingway, have generally and quite rapidly become popular writers, and the strongest new talents of the last few decades have leaped at once into popular favour without any intermediation of an avant-garde. I am thinking, for instance, of Dylan Thomas, Arthur Koestler and Tennessee Williams who have found immediately a multitude of readers; and at the moment there do not appear to be many young writers of first-rate promise for an avant-garde to bring forward. One of the editors of *New World Writing* says that in the last few years "avant-garde" has ceased to be a "meaningful term" because there is "no longer a recognizable . . . group of writers leading the rest in a genuinely new movement in literature." Something similar seems to be the case in England. Stephen Spender says that the youngest generation of English painters regard avant-garde movements as "old-fashioned." If this is true, it seems to suggest that the avant-garde is merging in the main body of the intellectuals again.

*
* *

However, for practical purposes one must assume that the avant-garde still exists, for at least the traces of it are all about us; though we must not confuse it with

the main body of the intellectuals, of which it forms
only a part. As for this main body,—whatever we may
think of the avant-garde,—we must be more careful
than ever not to attack it, for its members are now
the "eggheads" of the groundlings. When reactionary
forces are in power, as they are at present, the true
intellectuals must stand together, the "priests of the
mind" of Julien Benda who "seek their joy in the
practice of an art or a science or metaphysical specu-
lation." I mean the intellectuals who, in Padraic
Colum's phrase, conceive it to be their privilege and
duty to "write in favour of that which the great interests of the world are against." As Chekhov said in one
of his notes, "The power and salvation of a people
lie in its intelligentsia, in the intellectuals who think
honestly, feel and can work."

*

* *

I remember when these words first came into common
use, soon after avant-garde became a literary term.
"Intelligentsia" was a word we borrowed from the
Russians. In Russia it denoted the educated class who
had joined the ranks of the workers to become their
strategists and their tacticians and whose mission, as
Bertram D. Wolfe has observed, was "to be critics of

the world in which they had no place and prophets of a world that had not yet come into being." In Russia the intelligentsia were the leaven of the people, with whom they felt themselves deeply connected, and it was this conception of them that Julien Benda defended in France when he spoke, in a much discussed book, of the "Trahison des Clercs." What was this "treason of the intellectuals" that Julien Benda so deplored while defining the conscience and function of the intellectual class? It was their defection from the ideas of the Revolution that had actuated the Russian intelligentsia also. Their treason consisted in the "denial of progress," in "refusing to believe in any possible betterment of the soul of mankind," while they set up "the dogma of the incurable wickedness of men," together with a "romanticism of pessimism" and a "romanticism of contempt." As Benda said, "By feeling contempt for others" they obtained the "pleasure of a lofty attitude"; and in these respects our avant-garde,—or so it seems to me,—has been at one with Benda's "treasonable clerks." In this country, as it happens, the main intellectual body continues, on the whole, to defend the Revolution, the ideas of the Enlightenment that Benda defended,—or so I am persuaded as I read F. C. S. Northrop, Crane Brinton and Herbert J. Muller, the author of *The Uses of the Past*.

For all these three typically American thinkers agree
in feeling that, as one of them says, "We are still
children of the Enlightenment," still believing, after
two world wars, "in some form of progress," still convinced that the world can be changed for the better.
They maintain the Pelagian optimism of the American
tradition against the neo-Augustinian belief in the
depravity of man that has become dominant again in
theological circles. It is only our avant-garde that is,
or has been, treasonable, if we are to follow Julien
Benda, who was not surprised that the "romantic pes-
simists" appeal to the "elegant herd," since the words
"humanitarian" and "altruistic" are unquestionably
"boring."

*

* *

But is it not odd that the "Great Betrayal" of three or
four decades ago, when Julien Benda himself was a
hero of *The Dial,* should have become the actual boast
of our own contemporary avant-garde who think of
themselves as intellectuals *par excellence?* In reality,
they are detached as much from the parent intellectual
body as from any other body of the population, and
they knowingly occupy a sort of magic island that has
no connection with the mainland of American think-

ing. Nor do they stand for the cultural diversity that is so greatly needed now in the face of the leaden uniformity of the general mind, for they represent a still more reactionary orthodoxy, an authoritarian "system" that parallels the dogmatic religions. What Benda said is true today in the academic circles that are so largely governed by this avant-garde, "The man of letters who flies any political flag is obliged to wave the flag of 'order' if he wishes to obtain favours." Producing their own "reactionary essays," they echo the totalitarian leader who said, "Death to all who are not of our crowd," permitting no more deviation than any totalitarian permits and enforcing their own conformity for the same reason. What this leader felt they feel, "We dare not fail. That is why we must be merciless to our opponents. Those who even think of opposing us must be extirpated from the roots."

*

* *

In other words, the avant-garde are the "Initiated" of our time who parallel those of the ancient mystery religions, and they too cast out the "Uninitiated," regardless of personal merits. Just so the great Epaminondas was consigned to torment, while Pataikion, the "Initiated" burglar, went to everlasting bliss, all of which seemed as natural to the insiders as it seemed preposterous to those outside. Hence we have the well-known avant-garde "party line" which advances, at one moment, this poet or that, at another moment "going native," with the master list of authors that is ordained from above by those whose tastes are imposed and never questioned. From one end of the country to another one recognizes this party line the moment one enters avant-garde circles, just as one recognizes the master list. Hearing the name "John Donne" pronounced, one knows what is to follow,—James, Dante, Eliot, Melville, Joyce and so on. All other writers are excluded, and so are most readers. With the avant-garde, literature has become a "mysterious diversion of mandarins," a phrase of Jules Lemaître long ago. So it was also in the days when Greece had lost its freedom in the "literary hen-coops" of Alexandria, as Sir John Mahaffy called them.

*

* *

But what is the secret of the power that is exercised by this avant-garde and how do its members hold their position? They evidently perform a function in the American world we know, among the sensitive young, among literary students; and I think the clue to this can be found in what is often called the loneliness of just these types in our huge country. I was struck not long ago by a note about the author in one of the issues of *New World Writing*, "Mr. J. lives in R., Illinois, where he was born and educated." That seemed to me a revolutionary statement, for thirty years ago this writer would never have stayed in the town where he was born,—he would have escaped somehow to Paris or to Greenwich Village.

I know this, for I was a publisher's reader and read a novel every day in which some young man or woman did so. Having no "literary contacts" at home, he was driven to fly from the "sinking feeling that there is no use in it all . . . the general fate of talents in this country," as a friend of mine, a poet, wrote from the particular Winesburg where he committed suicide later. But now when, in the old sense, there is no Paris or Greenwich Village and only Rome has the necessary glamour of a refuge, more and more stay in the locales of the novels which they write. Malcolm Cowley has described these in *A Tidy Room in Bedlam* as a lonely ranch in Colorado, a village in East Texas, a small town in Georgia, a plantation house in the deep South or some college in the South, East or West.

Some of these locales have certainly changed in

thirty years but not enough to explain why the sensitive young no longer feel driven to get away; and it is surely not because, like Descartes in Amsterdam, they rejoice in the fact that as aliens they are ignored there. Descartes' reason for living in a foreign country was almost the definition of a strong confident talent. No, conditions have not greatly changed, nor are these young writers towers of strength. What keeps them then in their Winesburgs, alive, producing? Is it not the fact that the avant-garde provides them with the "literary contacts" that my friend, the poet, could not find three decades ago?

*

* *

For, with its chain of critical reviews and the summer writers' conferences that are also largely in its hands, it affords a life-line for the sensitive young, a sort of national "hook-up" that brings them into relation with a powerful circle. Insecure as they may be, personally low in vitality, they gain in self-confidence and strength by this connection, by this defensive alliance against a Philistine world that constitutes a kind of brotherhood. Or one might call it a secret society in which these lonely souls hold hands, as it were, from coast to coast, feeling that they are members of a true

élite who are both "of one's time" and "in the know."
In their *petite chapelle,* surrounded by their palisade,
they can write "pure" poetry, criticism, fiction, ignoring the world in which they live and which no longer
menaces them because they are insiders now in a larger
sphere. Since for them literature has ceased to be an
expression of society, they too have ceased to be obliged
to reflect the world; and they can play a sort of literary
solitaire in which psychological puppets serve for real
people. Young critics who have not won their spurs
can become authorities over-night by analyzing in
some new fashion a few lines of Dante, or they can
destroy in the eyes of their students,—thanks to the
glamour that teaching has acquired,—the life-work of
serious writers who are outside the party. Why should
they object to the central control that destroys their
independence, inasmuch as they have won security
by giving this up? "Timid men," as Jefferson said,
"prefer the calm of despotism to the boisterous sea of
liberty," and writers have many reasons to be timid
in our time.

*

* *

I have always liked Walt Whitman's phrase, "Beware
of the literary cliques. Keep well in the general crowd."

But in wide areas of this country there is no "crowd," no large element of the population that is responsive to literary minds, the "general" literary element that Whitman knew. (For he was in constant correspondence with writers and their friends.) One must therefore join a clique if one is not to be left alone in circumstances that are anything but fertilizing, in towns where one no longer finds the socialist "locals" of old that were once cosmopolitan centres of new learning and light. It is no wonder that the sensitive young flock to the universities, those islands of the relatively blest in a sea of troubles, where, thanks to the presence of the formalist critics and the poets who are allied to them, teaching has won so much prestige in literary circles. No wonder that the avant-garde plays such a role in this academic world, conferring as it does such benefits, so that, by means of it, even the weakest gain strength by combination and the humblest gain in self-esteem. It furnishes mutual reassurance and corroboration; and the more exclusive it enables one to be the more important one becomes, not only in one's own eyes but in the eyes of the party. So the more, in a big empty hostile world, the members can feel they are somebodies, the more fiercely they defend the party line and the more, at any price, they maintain their stockade, gladly accepting the kind of authority that is, or has been, antipathetic,—instinctively,—to Americans on every level.

*

* *

This literary conjuncture of our moment might have been predicted, and one might call any conjuncture good that enables the sensitive young to survive among untoward circumstances. If writers can live where they exist, and if they can be solitary without being at the mercy of hateful surroundings, is not that in our time sufficiently a triumph to vindicate any conditions that lie behind it? In this turbulent epoch of world revolution, when the problems of life and society seem too complex and enormous for the mind to cope with, one understands why writers, like Plato's wise men in the storm, stand aside under a wall for shelter. How natural at such times to seal oneself way from life, to escape from emotions and affections in abstractions and symbols, teaching literature in terms of itself rather than in terms of humanity and emptying it more and more of its vital content. For the rest, what a dry reservoir the human tradition has become since T. E. Hulme, that early avant-gardist, drained off "the sloppy dregs of the Renaissance," since Ezra Pound "chucked out" Thucydides and Virgil and Joyce satirized out of existence so many of the greatest writers with *all* the romantics. (Not, to be sure, for those who could discount the satire, but for countless graduates of "two-teacher high schools" who had scarcely heard of literature or art until they leaped straight into Picasso and Henry James, just as the Bismarck Islanders were said to have leaped directly out of the Stone Age into the Age of the Atom.) The humanist heritage of the literary mind has been narrowed down to the vanishing point by a generation that began with Dadaism and ended by virtually cleaning the slate of all that humanity has said and thought since the days of Shakespeare or even Dante. Similarly, literature itself,—or that which is guided by the avant-garde,—has virtually wiped humanity off the slate also, abandoning to the "middlebrow" writers the great subject-matter that has been the staple of the classics.

*

* *

Historically speaking, this is a phase, and we all know it is destined to pass, the question being, What is to succeed it? When a book was published not long ago called *Stories in the Modern Manner,* collected from an avant-garde magazine, one of the reviewers asked what trait the stories all possessed that justified this collective title "modern." It appeared that they all dealt with "the end of something, love, life, adolescence or illusion," and this reviewer's inference identified the avant-garde as a sort of continuation of the *fin de siècle.* Its characteristic note is the note of "last things,"—terminal, eschatological or what not—and it sings a perpetual swan-song over worlds of the past, befitting what Auden calls the epoch of the "Third Great Disappointment" when "a day is drawing to a close." But what is the next day going to be? For there must be other days. We are still in the dawn of history, in point of fact, and the world cannot die of old age at 12:01 in the morning, although after the disasters of the last forty years we can well understand why the notions of reason and progress have experienced a setback. Will the next phase be the return to mediæval notions that so many voices of our time have prophesied and fostered, that Eliot and Auden have equally favoured, with Joyce the mediævalist and Yeats who developed a hatred of everything modern? With Ezra Pound's *Cantos,* too, and even with D. H. Lawrence who said, "The great mass of humanity should never learn to read and write," a doctrine that must please the literary neo-scholastics who form so large a part of the avant-garde. Most of these minds have cherished the thought of a mediæval order in which the individual had a fixed place and was never permitted to question the presumptions of dogma, in which nonconformity was heresy and human nature was essentially bad and mankind was walled in forever by inevitable woe. Was it not of them that Toynbee was thinking when he followed Benda in reproaching the illuminati of our day for their "cynical loss of faith in the recently established principles" and their "nerveless surrender of the recently won gains, of Liberalism"? Yet these are the great imaginative spirits of the world-war epoch that have largely determined the outlook of the avant-garde, and thanks to them, at least in part, in our exhausted world, we seem indeed to be heading for another Middle Ages. We are almost as helpless as drunken men, overcome with sleep, who are trying to drive in the dark in a car without lights, and we are stupefied by the fumes of the spiritual monoxide gas that emanates from so much contemporary writing. Owing to the general loss of faith in civilization, in life, in man, we can scarcely keep awake, try as we will.

*

*   *

Meanwhile, the avant-garde, fostering "pure" poetry, fiction, art, withdrawing from the interests of society,

leaves these to the devil, so that the course of rebar-
barization which we are said to be following continues
unchecked by influences of the literary order. Never
has society needed more the aid and direction of the
literary minds which the avant-garde encourages to
stand aloof, viewing the concerns of mankind as none
of their business, so that many young writers look
blank now when anyone mentions the Dreyfus case
or refers to the American case of Sacco and Vanzetti.
"No causes,"—of any kind,—is one of their mottoes;
and they dwell fatalistically on the split between "mass
civilization" and "minority culture," phrases that have
become an incantation. (Not that the split does not
exist, but just how far does it exist at a time when so
many good writers find so many readers?) Yet these
young writers are not illiberal, whatever their teachers may be; they are full of a confused good will for
humankind; they simply do not see that their social
feeling has any connection with their work. Their
literary and their social selves travel in different directions, as if they were separate entities with nothing in
common; and does this not suggest that the avant-
garde lessons which they have been taught are at odds
with their new-world instincts and prepossessions?
These instincts continue to reflect the views of the
Enlightenment, the faith in reason, progress and

humankind that is "at bottom still *our* view of life," as Crane Brinton says in *Ideas and Men,* but they are benumbed and sterilized by the influence of the avant-garde, which is both anti-liberal and anti-humanistic. In consequence, the sensitive young, perplexed and divided, are "conservatively inclined" but "regretful" and "uncertain," words that especially apply to them, though used by a recent English writer to describe the general American mind of the present.

*
* *

In a word, owing to the avant-garde, a large part of our literature might be described as peripheral rather than central. It is the expression of a small closed world, walled in from the common world, which does not even wish to contribute to life, a semi-private art or game for which a great deal may be said but which is not a "literature fit for our occasions." (For what a role our literature might play in the emerging "planetary" world, the role that Whitman himself foresaw or dreamed of.) Will not our next phase restore this central literature, combining the great subject-matter of the "middlebrow" writers with the technical expertness bequeathed by the formalist critics, restoring in turn the notion of literature as a mirror and guide of society which is now discounted as journalistic?

One might well expect this, obvious as it must be that the avant-garde cannot produce this new departure, for, stifling both curiosity and independence, it does not permit the deviations that open new epochs. With its fanatical concentration on a few fashionable authors, it conveys no sense of the diversity of the history of letters, no feeling for the resources of the past that might breed fresh beginnings. For new departures one must look to the world outside the avant-garde, which inherits the exhaustion and despair of a diminished Europe, formed as it was under the spell of old-world writers for whom mankind had come to the end of its tether.

*

*   *

Or might there be a coup d'état within the avant-garde restoring its lost tie with the main intellectual body, with those who have never been guilty of the "treason" to the cause of liberalism that Julien Benda and Toynbee have equally lamented? This would be the best conjuncture, for anything else might jeopardize the avant-garde machinery that has been a blessing, with its magazines and summer conferences, for the sensitive young, while the avant-garde only half answers the needs of American writers, who cannot feel deeply involved in the "decline of the West." No more than the Asiatics, whose own world is beginning anew, can they share truly the European mood of the moment, the *fin de siècle* mood of the post-war epoch; for their country is too vigorous for this and it has lost too little. So one might suppose the time has come to accept Melville's injunction that America should "set, not follow, precedents," speaking not for the country that is but for the country that promises to be, even if it always breaks its word.

INDEX

INDEX

p. 118 History